Sagas

Finding faith after fifty

Sagas - Finding faith after fifty
© 10Publishing 2012 D.J. Carswell (Reprinted 2012, 2014)

Published in 2012 by 10Publishing, a division of 10ofthose.com

9D Centurion Court, Farington, Leyland, PR25 3UQ, England

Email. info@10ofthose.com
Website: www.10ofthose.com

ISBN 978-1-906173-29-6

Unless otherwise indicated, all Scripture quotations are taken from
the Holy Bible: New International Version.
Copyright © 1973, 1978, 1984 by International Bible Society.

Some of the names in this book have been changed, though all
the stories are true. Every effort has been made to ensure that all
quotations have been properly referenced and permission sought.
If further permissions are required for further editions please
contact the publisher who will endeavour to bring these about
for future editions.

Design and Typeset by Diane Bainbridge
Printed and bound by CPI Group (UK) Ltd, Croydon, CR0 4YY

STORIES OF CHANGED LIVES

D.J.CARSWELL

DEDICATED TO

Bettie Dedman and the late Bob Dedman, and David and Mary Hawthorne, who first introduced me to the God of the Bible.

CONTENTS

ACKNOWLEDGEMENTS

I was 'young' when I first started writing this book, and now I am a pensioner with a bus pass!

I am grateful to all who have allowed their story to be told in this book. Their desire and mine is that this book would be of help to anyone who wishes to find faith in God, especially those over the age of 50.

My sincere thanks go to everyone at 10 Publishing, especially Jonathan, Julia Cameron and Sheila Jacobs.

I am also deeply indebted to my husband, Roger, and family members for their input and encouragement to put pen to paper, or rather fingers to keyboard.

INTRODUCTION

REMEMBERING THE PAST – FACING THE FUTURE

The over-fifties are a very mixed bunch. The ever-increasing number in the UK come in all shapes and sizes, rich and poor, some energetic, some in pain, from all walks of life, but the majority wanting to make the most of their lives while running out of time.

Everyone who has managed to clock up half a century naturally will have formed opinions on most things, including faith and God. Of course we are always right, aren't we? And yet … what *do* we believe? And does it matter?

Sagas is a collection of real-life stories of mature people who have experienced something that has changed their outlook on life and death. Their honest, yet differing, accounts offer very personal insights into finding faith in the God of the Bible after the age of 50.

Older people in churches have often come to faith in their younger years, but not everyone has. It is sobering to realize that the choices we make about faith early on invariably shape our life on earth and in eternity.

This book shows, however, that it is not too late to change. I hope that it might answer some of your questions, dispel doubts or help you to come to faith. Each story stands alone so you can start at the beginning or pick random chapters. Most of the stories are fairly short but one account is deliberately longer than the others, as it is about a famous man whose face is instantly recognizable – Colonel Sanders. His background is fascinating, unusual and yet most people know little about him.

Running through each story is the thread of 'grace'. In poetry, this has been expressed so clearly in the lines of the well-known song 'Amazing Grace', written by a former slave trader, whose life story is also included.

So let me introduce you to a few people who, while remembering the past and facing the future, have found faith in God.

D.J. Carswell

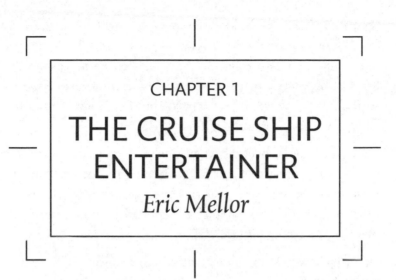

CHAPTER 1

THE CRUISE SHIP ENTERTAINER

Eric Mellor

The Saga generation is a very mixed bunch. Whilst some may be coping with the intricacies of stair lifts, others are up in snowy mountains negotiating ski lifts! Depending on health and wealth, over-fifties often lead full and active lives for far longer than their parents and grandparents ever did. Despite the memories of the ill-fated *Titanic* ship, cruises have over the years proved popular, especially with older passengers.

Eric Mellor was born on 23 October 1910, in Salford, into a home that loved music and was full of musicians. His great-grandfather mastered the large double bass to such a level that he played in the Bournemouth Municipal Orchestra (now the Bournemouth Symphony Orchestra). Eric's father inherited the musical talent, resulting in him becoming a professional musician. No doubt growing up in a somewhat austere musical atmosphere had an effect on Eric, which meant that he too would have to practice for hours daily on a chosen instrument.

Back then, families would gather together just to sing. Even in the 'picture houses' the films at first were silent, and thus totally reliant upon a piano player to musically set the scenes. As all Eric's family played, they were each called upon at various times to perform this very important task. The Mellors also possessed a very large classical musical library.

Eric, inevitably, became a professional musician. Most of his life was spent either touring or playing in various resident orchestras and bands. If you had been on the original *Queen Mary* cruise ship, you might have spotted a violinist or bass player as the young Mr Eric Mellor.

During these touring times, Eric not only had an ear for music but an eye for a girl – a certain Betty Wilson, with whom he fell in love. Betty was an attractive dancer, whose colourful personality somehow even put Eric in the shade.

In the 1940s, Eric was a bass player in the residential Pavilion Theatre Orchestra, Bournemouth, continuing what was to be a generation-by-generation association with the seaside town.

Eric would be envied by some who looked at his lifestyle, the glamour of the cruise ship, and the accolade given at his performances. He was without doubt a real character who was loved by everyone, especially his children, Mike and Irene.

Mike had found a job in the newspaper business, but in the evenings he was out playing in bands at various gigs. Alcohol featured prominently in his life, which was set on a downward spiral and would have ended in tragedy if something amazing hadn't happened. Through the witness of a colleague at the *Bournemouth Echo*, Mike became a Christian. He came to real faith in Jesus Christ as his personal Saviour. This totally transformed his life, his health, his family and his future. Eric and Betty were baffled. What on earth had happened to their trombone-playing son whose lifestyle had been causing them so many worries?

Always supportive as good parents, Betty first and then Eric were to come to understand and experience for themselves what had happened to Mike (and his wife) in relation to faith.

Mike explains: 'Mum came to trust in Christ and would often speak of the joy of knowing what it was to be forgiven. Dad remained unchanged, until something in his personal life caused him much inner regret and brokenness. It was this that led him also to a genuine repentance and personal trust in Jesus Christ.

'His was a simple faith. I remember his routine of making his porridge and reading his Bible. Morning by morning he would read, having started at the book of Genesis and slowly working his way through to Revelation and back again. His favourite verse contained the words of Jesus: "Peace I leave with you; my peace I give you. I do not give to you as the world gives. Do not let your hearts be troubled and do not be afraid" (John 14:27).

> **" The peace the world offers depends on having good health, or a good pension or good family and friends, but none of these are certain and may only be temporary. "**

'The peace the world offers depends on having good health, or a good pension or good family and friends, but none of these are certain and may only be temporary. Dad loved solitude, the countryside and his own company, but none of these can give deep, inner peace. Real peace comes from a guilt-free conscience. Mum had passed away before Dad, but he continued to be cheerful, content and humorous to the end.

'It is such a joy to know that because of his simple trust in Jesus, Dad – Mr Eric Mellor, a former cruise ship musician and member of a well-known orchestra, is in heaven. He is neither a star in the sky looking down on us, nor playing bass in the "St Peter's All Stars". He is "with Christ, which is better by far"' (Phil. 1:23).

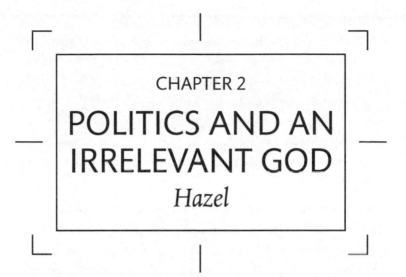

CHAPTER 2

POLITICS AND AN IRRELEVANT GOD
Hazel

Her grandfather was not pleased; rather, he was angry. As she climbed on to his knee to look at the picture book of the royal family which he held in his hands, Hazel's granddad muttered, 'I have to feed that lot before I can buy my own children a crust of bread!'

A silversmith by trade in the suburbs of London, her anti-monarchist grandfather had been forced to leave school at the age of 12 to look after his ailing mother.

'Our family,' recalls Hazel, 'was rather large, loving and full of aunts, cousins, grandparents and a wonderful mother and father. You could also describe us as working class, very radical, left wing and republican.' There was no mistaking that family's politics. They all worked tirelessly for the old Labour party.

'I spent many hours watching votes being counted in various elections at Brent Town Hall, cheering when we won and bemoaning our lot when we lost.'

All their neighbours were Jewish. There were the Levys, the Cohens and the Rothenburgs. I would baby-sit for Rabbi Rabinowitz. My father would regularly don his little skullcap to go and help the caretaker clean the chandeliers in the synagogue at the bottom of the road. There really was no animosity between us. As children, we all played together. We ate their smoked salmon and they ate our Christmas cakes. They built strange shelters in their gardens and we decorated our Christmas tree.

'So I was born into this vibrant, political, argumentative family. I was the eldest. Although I had all the love, care and encouragement that they could possibly give, there was one thing missing – there was no God. God wasn't mocked, He wasn't rejected; He was just an irrelevance. Our gods were the Labour Party and the TUC. Our devils were the Conservative Party and the employers. Our hope of resurrection was the eventual recognition of the worthiness of the working man. I was quite grown up before I realized that Conservatives actually could be nice people. I even married one!'

> **" God wasn't mocked, He wasn't rejected; He was just an irrelevance. Our gods were the Labour Party and the TUC. "**

Although Hazel was surrounded by such strong opinions, she alone in her family, and from an early age, knew that there was something more to life – a light to follow, an elusive something to be searched for, a truth to be known and held.

'Of course I knew the Lord's Prayer and hymns, because we had assembly at school and RE stories, but to me these were just words or history. They weren't real and they weren't personal.'

Even before she started secondary school, Hazel had three big, unanswered questions.

'When I was 9 years old, my baby sister, who was only 4, died of cancer. I remember looking at her little white coffin and thinking, "Where is she? Where has she gone? Where is the very essence of Judy now?" I suppose I meant her soul but I didn't know I did, and anyway, since no one close to me believed in God, nobody could tell me. Judy was dead and that was that. I still remember the desolation of my poor parents, but somehow I knew that this didn't have to be the end of the story. So that was my first question – what really happened when children died?

> " *Of course I knew the Lord's Prayer and hymns, because we had assembly at school and RE stories, but to me these were just words or history. They weren't real and they weren't personal.* "

'My paternal grandmother had lost her husband in the First World War, and then her son (my dad's younger brother) in World War Two. As a consequence of this she had flung herself into the activities of the British Legion. Because I loved her so much, I used to go with her on visits to the Royal Star & Garter Homes where I saw many injured people. I was never shielded from the ravages of war. My parents thought I should see what cruelty man could inflict on man because I was expected to grow up and make my contribution to a better world. My grandmother and I would go to special British Legion services at Westminster Abbey, where I would see many victims of the war. Of course I sang the hymns and prayed the prayers, but they were just words. I clearly remember looking at those

" There must be an answer to this unbearable suffering. "

broken men and weeping women and thinking, "There must be an answer to this unbearable suffering."

'The third was very ordinary. I was walking along my street, on my own. I was very content. The sky was blue, so blue and vivid that I suddenly wanted to shout out a great big thank you for the beautiful world and everything in it. But whom could I thank? No one could say.'

Hazel went on wondering but continued to get nowhere, finding no answers. Always in the back of her mind were questions and perplexities. 'There wasn't a Bible in the house, and anyway, I wouldn't have known to look for answers there.'

Leaving school, Hazel embarked on a course at a teacher training college. It was while she was there that she met a Christian who shared with her the good news that God loved her and sent His Son, Jesus, to die for her sins. 'I really didn't understand this, but it sort of opened the door a little for me to progress a step further.'

Soon it was all change, for Hazel met William, married him, and then moved up north. By then, she reasoned (wrongly she now knows) that if God did love her then she had to repay Him by being and doing good.

'So I involved myself in all the village activities. I blush with shame when I think back to those days. What a priggish, pious, sanctimonious life I lived for years. There wasn't anything I didn't help with. I ran a playgroup, Brownies and a youth club. I was secretary of the PCC, and I organized cheese and wine parties until I was bored to tears. Never once did I ask God if this was what He wanted me to do. I never opened a Bible. I never prayed. Of course I thought I was pleasing God. I was doing good, wasn't I? I was truly wonderful and I knew I was, because I told myself that on a daily basis. I was sacrificing myself for the good of the village, and they had better appreciate me.'

The hollowness, the emptiness inside Hazel grew and grew. She longed for spiritual sustenance, which she couldn't find, and all her good works never supplied.

'I didn't know what to do or where to go until one day the thought came to me, "Go along to the nearby chapel at Capernwray." God obviously thought I needed a good shove. Oh, I didn't want to. It was strange … and I would have to go on my own.'

Hazel did pluck up the courage to go along, and made the most amazing discovery – the answer to her questions. Only the answer was not a 'what' but a 'who'. As she listened to sermons and studied the Bible along with others, she slowly became acquainted with God.

'I remember with astonishment being told by a Christian friend to read the Bible, like other books, from beginning to the end. I thought, "What, even the Old Testament? Isn't that only for the Jews?"'

Hazel came to understand that it was her sin that was getting in the way of her knowing God personally. The only way to deal with that sin was not by doing her best or living a 'good' life. In fact there was nothing that she (or we) could do. God Himself provided the solution. The Easter hymn, 'There Is A Green Hill Far Away' has a verse which puts this truth succinctly:

There was no other good enough
To pay the price of sin;
He only could unlock the gate
*Of heaven, and let us in.**

Hazel was listening and reading with a heart that was agreeing with what she heard. One day, while peeling potatoes, she felt the desire to pray. 'OK, Jesus, I don't know much about You yet, but I am getting to know You. So I'll just say yes – yes, You are my Lord and Master, and I want You in my life.'

The once irrelevant God became the known God.

* 'There Is A Green Hill Far Away', Cecil Alexander, 1818–95.

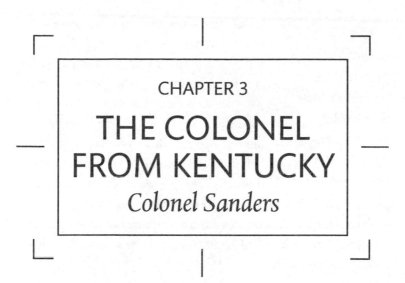

CHAPTER 3

THE COLONEL FROM KENTUCKY

Colonel Sanders

Colonel Sanders is famous throughout the world for his fast-food outlets, serving chicken cooked with its own special recipe. We all recognize his product and the logo of the Colonel himself – a genial, white-haired, moustached and bearded gentleman.

Harland Sanders was born in September 1890, near Henryville, Indiana in the USA. Although we know him as a successful franchise founder, during his lifetime he held a number of varied and surprising jobs. Despite his being a sixth-grade drop out, Harland was hardworking and not one to miss a trick. By the age of 12, he had become a farm hand. This young labourer then went on to become an army mule tender, a locomotive fireman, a railroad section hand, an aspiring lawyer, an insurance salesman, a ferryboat entrepreneur, Chamber of Commerce secretary, a tyre salesman, an amateur obstetrician, an unsuccessful political candidate, a petrol station and motel operator and, of course, a restaurateur.

> **" 'Mama', according to Harland, 'wouldn't take no monkey business from us kids.' "**

But first, tragedy was to strike the family. When he was only 5, Harland's father died. This came not long after his sister Catherine's birth. How immense was the task that his mother now had to undertake as she tackled raising the family alone. But 'Mama', according to Harland, 'wouldn't take no monkey business from us kids.' She was left with the responsibility of raising four children as well as looking after farmland, chickens, a pig and a cow. She not only made the children go to church and Sunday school, she set an example by taking them herself.

'Always tell the truth, don't cheat and be kind to each other. Be a man when you grow up. Don't touch alcohol or tobacco and remember card playing never did nobody no good.' These were some of her rules of life. Mama's training was so good that by the age of 7 Harland could bake a loaf of bread all by himself. Cooking would always be important to him, especially in later life.

Harland was fired from his first job. Not an auspicious start you might think, especially as he was ashamed at having to own up to his mother, who gave him a 'mouthful'. But it made him resolve to always do what he was called to do. He learned to like hard work.

It was not until a certain Mr Broaddus came on to the scene that changes came to the Sanders family. Mama knew him from when they were at school together. One day Mama announced to her family that soon he would be their new stepfather and that they would be moving to Greenwood, Indiana. After a while, it was apparent that things weren't working out quite as expected. Harland and his step-dad didn't get on. It also transpired that his mother was not finding life what she had anticipated. Things got so bad that Harland knew that he had to leave home. Mama gave him their only suitcase which was old and battered. Many tears were shed as he set off for a new work and a new life.

After a couple of years of farming and a job collecting fares for the streetcar company in New Albany, Harland met up with some army recruiters. He protested to one of them that he was only 16 so he wasn't eligible. 'Just tell them you are 21,' they said, 'and they'll take you.'

He did … and they did. But he had told a lie. No doubt he was haunted by his mother's words of advice to 'Always tell the truth' as soon he found himself, not in some cosy barrack on dry land, but on a boat that was riding a turbulent sea, heading for Cuba!

Harland reckoned that 'the only good thing about my getting into the army … was that I got out four months later. Even that was too long.'

Most young men Harland's age aspired to ride or even drive a locomotive. The railroad had arrived with its seemingly endless lines of track, which carried those fascinating steaming fiery engines; huge beasts needing constant supplies of coal to feed their insatiable appetite. Little wonder then that Harland really couldn't believe his good fortune when he landed a job emptying the ashes out of fireboxes. One morning, a fireman didn't show up for work, so would he like to fire the engine? He must have done a good job because the engineer offered him regular work. He was still only 16, so Mama had to sign the papers for him.

> **" I thought she was right pretty. An' after a few weeks, when I could see she was lookin' forward to seein' me when I come to Jasper, I reckoned it was time to ask her to marry me. "**

The romance of the railroad was not the only thing that stirred Harland's young heart. After the thrill of roaring through towns, people waving and him working amid dirt, oil and steam, Harland would 'chill out' at an old-fashioned picture house. He freely admitted that the pictures weren't up to much. But there was nowhere else for a young man to spend his time. One night he encountered Josephine King outside the theatre.

'I thought she was right pretty. An' after a few weeks, when I could see she was lookin' forward to seein' me when I come to Jasper, I reckoned it was time to ask her to marry me.'

Wasting no time, they set up home in Tuscumbia in Alabama. Reflecting on that time some years later, Harland commented, 'We'd have done a whole lot better if we'd stayed round the church more in them days. But we was young and it seemed like there was other things to do than goin' to church. So we just didn't – somethin' I learned to regret in the years to come ...'

The railroad jobs with which Harland became involved meant that he was separated for much of the time from his family.

It was a fist fight that lost him his job at Illinois Central. No one would have guessed that his next way of making money would be through the law. Harland had been studying the subject by correspondence. A nasty railroad incident enabled him to use the skills he had acquired to deal with power of attorney statements enabling passengers to claim compensation. He was beginning to feel that maybe he was meant to be a lawyer. A judge allowed him to use his law library. Harland began to practice in the Justice of Peace Court. Fortunately for him, there was no rule that said he had to be admitted to the bar to practice, so that was how he got by. Most of the claims were relatively minor, but one day an incident with a loan shark ultimately led to changes in legislation, which put Harland out of a job – again.

Whilst falling back on railroading, plus some escapades putting his brother Clarence into barbering, Harland couldn't help but notice that some of his cousins went around dressed in white collars and suits. Since they came from the same stock as him Harland fancied that he, too, could leave behind the overalls and railroad cap and begin a new career in insurance. By now he was the father of two girls and a boy. As well as supporting his own family, he wanted to be able to help his mother who was alone back in Indiana.

In true Harland Sanders style he gave his new job everything he had. Working all hours, and with some unusual methods, Harland sold his insurance. In thirteen months he was promoted to assistant superintendent. But inevitably, it wasn't long before he began to hit trouble. Rules and regulations always seemed to figure somewhere in his demise, even though he felt he was doing what was fair and right by his bosses. Somehow Harland managed to find time to found a Young Businessmen's Club. Less respectably, he also became embroiled in a fight with the town tough, who made it his business to bully the people of Jeffersonville.

The next venture involved 'Old Asthma'. 'She was a wood-hulled, sternwheeler ferryboat that crossed the river at Jeffersonville – but only when conditions suited her. She wheezed like she had asthma; that's how she got her name. She was as undependable as she was noisy. She couldn't run in winter because of the floating ice.'

One of the most profound influences on Harland's life was the Rotary Club. Their slogans impressed him: 'He profits most who serves best' and 'Service before self'. 'That implied real service. You just give unselfishly to anybody – in your business and everywhere else. That just seemed to fit what I wanted to be and do.'

A few years later, the Rotary Club brought in the Four-Way Test:

1. Is it the truth?
2. Is it fair to all concerned?
3. Will it build goodwill and better friendships?
4. Will it be beneficial to all concerned?

Harland was of the opinion that unless a man could abide by that test, then he didn't think he would amount to very much.

Life was never dull for Harland. He even nearly died when he was driving his car over a bridge, which collapsed beneath him. With two black eyes, a sore head and no car he was back looking for new employment again.

"You might think that I was discouraged at this point, but I wasn't. I just believed that any failure I had gave me the opportunity to start over again or try something new."

'I went to Nicholasville and began what probably marked one of the most important turns in my career.'

He took over and reopened a petrol station. Soon he had a

thriving business, which continued for a long time, until the historical stock market crash and a drought hit.

'Everybody was broke.' He went on, 'You might think that I was discouraged at this point, but I wasn't. I just believed that any failure I had gave me the opportunity to start over again or try something new.'

Shell Oil Company in Middlesboro, Kentucky, offered to build him a petrol station in Corbin, Kentucky. They would charge no rent. So naturally, he accepted. This decision pre-empted what was to become one of the world's most enterprising entrepreneurial ventures of the last century.

An idea came to Harland as he realized that traffic was building up on the route that passed his place. As they were mostly truckers, he reasoned that they would likely need to stop for food, a rest and conveniences. The old family dining table was wheeled out, along with six chairs, and placed in a cleaned-up corner that had been previously used for storage. The plan was for the food to be ready for 11 o'clock. If enough customers turned up and ate all the food, that was fine. The family would just make some more later. If only a few showed up, then they would eat what they had prepared anyway! So, in his first 'restaurant' everyone shared the same table; but no one seemed to mind, as the food was so good. All the time he was trying to think of new ways to satisfy his customers. This ensured that they would come back, and also attract new ones.

Undoubtedly, Harland was having an eventful life. By nature, he seemed to be a very generous man, always wanting to help his neighbours, and he loved children, especially showing sympathy in a practical way toward those who came from broken homes and those without parents. Many of his good deeds seemed to resemble Christian virtues, but he confessed, 'I knew I wasn't livin' for God.' He readily admitted that God was good to him, especially when he had a few 'close calls'. Each time he believed that God had pulled him through. 'Seems … to me God was either gettin' ready to punish me real good, or he was savin' me to use me.'

The business was expanding. New premises and membership of the National Restaurant Association were the order of the day. Harland had ideas, took risks and was a savvy negotiator when it came to finance. He had a seventeen-bed motel built next to his restaurant, plus plans for another some ninety miles away at a tourist resort, when disaster struck. Fire partially destroyed his premises at Corbin. Initially, he thought he would just stick with the motel and not rebuild the restaurant. It was a lot of trouble getting the right chef, waitresses, and upholding good food and hygiene standards. But then the thought came to him, 'You can sleep a man only once in twenty-four hours but you can feed him three times.'

A new restaurant was built, seating 140 people. From then on he decided that his future was to be in food, not motels.

Life must have seemed good; but life also has that ability to throw the unexpected, and often unpleasant, things our way. His 20-year-old son died from blood poisoning. The business in Asheville had to close because of food rationing during World War Two. The Great Depression, which was also followed in the States by drought, affected business. A project he had started was to open an airport nearby. But a couple of plane crashes sealed its fate.

He also had an unhappy marriage, ending when his wife divorced him after thirty-nine years.

Although he never intended to marry again, he eventually married Claudia, one of his earlier employees. After being married for twenty-five years to Claudia, he made this remark: 'I've taken good care of Josie [his ex-wife]. She's never wanted for a thing. She owns a home, which I gave her, and she's got money in the bank. She visits in my home, and is always welcomed in our company.'

Harland had suffered losses. Even his place at Corbin had been auctioned for less than he had been offered not that long before. The amount raised barely paid his taxes and outstanding bills. At 65 years of age, some men, having had a busy life, might think of settling down to enjoy the fruits of their labours. Harland found that his was a different scenario. 'I had my social security cheque to live on. But that was about all, and that wasn't very much.' What was he to do?

Harland Sanders could fry chicken. It tasted good. Very good indeed. Although his regulars really liked his recipe, he decided to try a little change in the herbs and spices. The chicken was so delicious that the recipe has never changed. Kentucky Fried Chicken had arrived!

The idea came to him that he should franchise his recipe. Sanders also did something that a lot of people do when they don't know what to do next or are just in a desperate situation. He prayed.

'While I wasn't right with God, I remember prayin' to God the Almighty,

> **" You've helped me in the past, and I need Your help now, God. And I promise You, if this idea of franchising works out because of Your blessing, You'll get your share.**"

"You've helped me in the past, and I need Your help now, God. And I promise You, if this idea of franchising works out because of Your blessing, You'll get your share.'"

Pete Harman was a chap he knew from the National Restaurant Association. Sanders wondered if he might be interested in his way of doing chicken. 'When you are in the restaurant business you're always looking for some kind of speciality dish that you can offer which will prove an attraction to your customers and yet is something your competitor doesn't have.'

Sanders had been invited to visit Pete's place, and somehow managed to get round to serving up his very own special fried chicken. And Pete, in a passing remark, referred to Sanders as 'Colonel'.

Harland had only stopped off for a short time as he was on his way to Australia where he hoped he would find some inspiration at a religious convention to overcome his 'cussin', which bothered him. On his return, Claudia, his wife, took him back to Pete's place. There in bold letters on the front of the restaurant were the words 'Kentucky Fried Chicken – Something New Something Different'.

From this inauspicious beginning came the launch of marketing the franchising of the famous recipe. Of course, there were disappointments when influential people showed no interest. There were long hours travelling, (sometimes sleeping nights in the back of the car), negotiating, and also mixing those spices. One of the things that kept him going was that he knew he had a strong product.

The method of cooking the chicken was vital. Any process that took too long would find the customer leaving early. French-frying could make the chicken dry, crusty or unevenly done.

'Colonel Sanders, why not try a pressure cooker?' suggested a man from the local hardware store.

'It took me a while experimenting to get the right balance of cooking time, pressure and amount of fat. But finally with my secret recipe of eleven spices and herbs, which is still used today by all Kentucky Fried Chicken outlets, I was able to come up with a method of sealing in the chicken flavour, preserving its moisture, and giving it a soft finish that just melts in your mouth.'

> **" But finally with my secret recipe of eleven spices and herbs, which is still used today by all Kentucky Fried Chicken outlets, I was able to come up with a method of sealing in the chicken flavour, preserving its moisture, and giving it a soft finish that just melts in your mouth."**

Restaurants would invite Harland and his wife to demonstrate their famous chicken. She would greet the customers, give out the menus and tell them something about the food they were about to sample. Meanwhile, Harland would be in the kitchen doing all the cooking. Later, he would do the 'coloneling' … putting on a waistcoat, long-tailed coat and gold watch chain before going to chat with the customers.

> **" By 1960 Colonel Sanders had about two thousand restaurants in the United States and six in Canada. Three years later there were 600 and they had become the largest fast-food franchiser in the country. "**

Up until this time, people had affectionately calling him 'Colonel'. In 1935 the state governor had given him the honorary title of 'Kentucky Colonel', which Harland presumed was because of his reputation for good food and service to the community. Thus came about the slogan 'Colonel Sanders Recipe Kentucky Fried Chicken'. Then came the moustache. And the goatee beard.

And the cane. The white suit came later. It was because he always liked to look clean; even back in his railroad days he would wear white overalls and white cotton gloves.

By 1960 Colonel Sanders had about two thousand restaurants in the United States and six in Canada. Three years later there were 600 and they had become the largest fast-food franchiser in the country. The idea of a takeaway product came from something his daughter said. She didn't want to own her own restaurant; she would rather have a place where people came for ready cooked food and took it away with them.

The first free-standing building to sell Kentucky Fried Chicken was put up in Jacksonville, Florida by Wally Desser. It was a model for everything that has been done since.

Although Colonel Sanders appeared to be a decent figure in his signature suit, was well thought of in his community and gave to charity and good causes, something always troubled him. He could never give up 'cussin', which he knew his mother would never approve of, let alone a Holy God. A white suit could not get rid of a guilty conscience. In his book, published in 1974,* he reveals his inner thoughts and what happened to him in his later years.

I always gave money to the church or religious causes. That was good.

What wasn't good was my cussin'. I learned this when I worked on the railroad as a boy. And I polished up on it in later years. Cussin' was just my way of expressing myself. One man told me he never knew there were so many cuss words in the English language. That's the kind of reputation I had, you see.

Now I knowed this wasn't good for me, because the older I got – when I thought about it, the more I realized that I had no faith in God. Yes, I believed there was a God. But I didn't have the assurance that He was with me, because I knew I wasn't with Him ... this bothered me.

All my life I've tried to help people ... I wasn't much for churchgoin' like most religious folks. I believed in God, all right. And I believe He was on my side, but somehow it didn't seem like I was on His side. That weren't His fault either. He tried to get my attention a number of different times.

Harland had two encounters involving Scientology and horoscopes, which affected him:

I knew the Bible doesn't have anything too good to say about wizards and soothsayers. And I don't want to have nothing to do with anything the Bible is against and God don't approve of ... They was a reminder to me that man is a part of something a lot bigger than himself. If God created the world – and I know He done that – and I am part of His creation, then I should have a close relationship with Him. I didn't and it bothered me ... all the success I'd had with my franchising business and all the recognitions, awards, and honours that came to me still left me with a hollow feelin'.

... I was a good citizen and all that. But all this while I knew I wasn't right with God. It bothered me especially when I'd take the name of the Lord in vain.

Then one day I was walkin' along the street in Shelbyville when two men come along. They stopped me and one of them said he was pastor of Evangel Tabernacle in Louisville. He introduced me to the other man, Rev. Colman McDuff. 'We're having evangelistic services at our church this week, Colonel. Mr McDuff and his brother are preaching. We'd like to invite you to attend.' 'Thank you,' I said, 'but I'm very busy these days.' As I recall, they gave me a little card or a piece of paper tellin' about the meetings, and I went on my way home.

I was about to forget about the whole dang thing when I thought to myself, 'Here I am afraid of dyin' because of my cussin'. I've already gone a halfway round the world to Australia to try to get help, and here these fellows are just askin' me to come across town.'

So a couple of nights later I walked into the Evangel Tabernacle. I'd never been before. Rev. Rodgers was standing at the door greeting everyone. 'Glad to have you here, Colonel. I'd like you to sit upon the platform with me during the opening period of our service.' 'Oh no, I can't do that,' I said.

'You might as well. Everybody will be lookin' at you. And if you sit up there, they can all see you. We'll take a seat down in the front when the preacher starts,' he said.

Well, that sounded logical to me ... it was an interestin' service, as I recall, with lots of music. I'd never heard such enthusiastic singing before.

Then Rev. McDuff preached his sermon.

When the reverend finished his message, anybody who wanted to ask Jesus Christ to come into their life was asked to raise their hand to indicate their decision.

This was what I had been wantin' all my life. So I put up my hand. I think the reverend suggested we kneel down ...

'Do you think a man can get enough religion, or have an experience with God, so he'll know he'll go to heaven when he dies?' I asked him.

'Yes. You surely can. The Bible says, "If you confess with your mouth that Jesus is Lord, and believe in your heart that God raised Him from the dead, you will be saved.'

That was exactly what he wanted.

He said that he would pray a little prayer and that if I was to repeat it after him and really mean it then he was sure that God would hear me and accept me.

I believe the prayer went something like this:

'Lord, I'm a sinner. I need You as my Saviour. I really mean this prayer, Lord, and I pray in Jesus' name.'

You know, it just seemed like a great burden was lifted off my shoulders. I'd never felt anything like that before, and here I was seventy-nine years old.

The Colonel was still bothered by something, so he asked the reverend another question: 'Can God help me stop cussin'?' 'He certainly can,' came back the reply from the preacher. He pointed him to a verse in the Bible that says, 'Therefore I tell you, whatever you ask for in prayer, believe that you have received it, and it will be yours' (Mark 11:8).

So I prayed again and asked the Almighty to help me stop misusin' His name. And I'll say this, when I walked out of that church that night I knew I was a different man. I had met God ... All my tithing and good deeds had never given me the sense of God's presence that I knew then. And that feelin' has never left me.

Colonel Sanders had become a real Christian, believing that Jesus died bearing the punishment for his sins and that because of Jesus' resurrection, a way had been made for people to get right with God. He was afraid of dying before and that he wouldn't go to heaven. Now he was right with God, who gave him a peace that success and money never could. He also honoured his pledge to 'give God His share'.

Eventually other businessmen came along and were entrusted with the famous brand name and product. Harland was pleased that he had created jobs for people, produced a fine recipe enjoyed by millions worldwide, and had made others rich. He probably could have made far more money, but his priorities were to work hard and always to give his best to help people get more out of life.

And to all those who are facing retirement he passed on some wise advice:

I think you should plan your retirement, not as though you are bein' deprived of somethin' but with a spirit of havin' somethin' added to your life. You see, you are not startin' out from nothin', but from the point at which you have assimilated the lessons of a lifetime. Those years are sort of the crown you wear as you begin the next phase of your life.

I pray to God Almighty my story will encourage you also to commit your life to Jesus. If you will, no matter what hard times you may go through – if you keep turning to Him, acknowledging Him, and honouring Him in all you do – He'll help you through.

Harland 'Colonel' Sanders died on 16 December 1980.

* *Colonel Harland Sanders, Life As I Have Known It Has Been Finger Lickin' Good (Florida: Creation House, 1974).*

CHAPTER 4
THE SOUNDS
OF MUSIC
Carolyn

Her family must have been hedging their bets when it came to religion. Carolyn was baptized as an infant by her uncle who was a canon at Sheffield Cathedral. The Methodists were next on the list, but this time it was for Sunday school where she enjoyed singing hymns. Then it was time for the Roman Catholic Church. 'When I was 4 years old, my parents decided to send me to a Roman Catholic convent school as a day pupil. To this day, I have no idea why, except that my father, who is a stickler for discipline in schools, having been a head teacher himself, perhaps thought this was needed for a 4-year-old! The nuns were great and I loved every minute. We were encouraged, from the start, to be involved in every aspect of convent life (as long as the nuns set the boundaries). I can remember being tested in the catechism from the earliest times each month by a very formidable priest …

We were always treated as part of the religious community.'

While growing up in the convent, Carolyn learned the music to sing at all the services – plainsong and in Latin – so there were numerous versions of the 'Ave Maria'. Reciting the rosary was part of the routine, together with prayers before each lesson in the various languages she learned, as well. In her teens, Carolyn discovered she had a flair for music. As a pianist, she began to study this at school, becoming more and more involved in its religious musical life.

'There has never been a time when I didn't believe in God, but as to having a personal relationship with Him, that was never an option. As far as I was concerned, He was remote, awesome and completely inaccessible through clouds of incense.'

The inevitable happened when she was 17. Carolyn announced to her parents that not only did she want to become a Roman Catholic, but also that she felt a 'call to the religious life'. She wanted to become a nun.

Carolyn elaborates: 'This was not because of biblical truth I had received, but rather the trappings of religious ritual.'

Understandably, her parents' reaction was one of shock and hurt. 'My parents were wonderful, but I was *Anglican*! I was also the kind of Anglican where God was kept at a distance … He didn't interfere with one's own life.'

Her parents didn't really know how to handle the situation, so they gave her a choice. Either she went to music college and stayed at home, or she pursued this new venture and left. 'Where was God now?' she pondered.

'Well, at 17, with no money to set up home, I chose to go to college, thereby proving that the religious vocation was not from God.'

Carolyn entered the Royal Manchester College of Music (now the Royal Northern) where she studied for five years, obtaining a music degree as well as performing and teaching. 'In my ignorance,' she says, 'I put God aside.' While at college she was sent on a travelling scholarship to the Mozarteum in Salzburg, Austria. Although this was a fantastic and privileged experience musically, she began to feel lonely in the evenings, wondering why her college friend, who was also awarded the music scholarship, was ill with cancer and therefore unable to be in Salzburg. This started her thinking about the big issues of life and, of course, God.

'Fortunately, God had never put me aside; in His infinite patience, He just waited.'

On returning home, a piano professor encouraged Carolyn to play the organ in a local Anglican church. 'At least it got me into a place of worship and I heard the Bible read. But there was never any real teaching of the Bible that would actually inspire me to read it when I got home. The vicar was good at jokes, though.'

Her job as director of piano studies in a girls' public school, as well as doing recital work, meant that she had links with a cathedral. As a result, she began attending the services.

'I was confirmed there, so God was revisited somehow, through the music, I think. But truly I was still in a fog spiritually – not the incense variety! I met my husband at this time and so was married there.

'Setting up home happened to be 100 yards from the local

church, and eventually I was asked to lead the choir and play the organ. I enjoyed it all, and also putting the choristers through the medal scheme of the Royal School of Church Music. My husband had been brought up in a Baptist church, so he was rather overwhelmed by all this Anglicanism and kept his head down, apart from Easter and Christmas. So here I was in a church environment where music was everything in my life. Doing things like that was knowing God, surely … How wrong I was.'

Something new began to happen at church. It led to Carolyn being encouraged to sing new worship songs and attend conferences, but she never actually read God's Word, the Bible – only books about 'renewal' and the Holy Spirit.

'I was really hoping something would happen by my efforts. How could I have been so ignorant and blind? I became an expert in all "churchy" things – candles, colour of vestments, read lessons; I sang; in fact I did everything there except stand in the pulpit. But still the Lord Jesus Christ and the Bible were at a distance – both undiscovered. I didn't consider the cross in personal terms at all, and looking back, I couldn't distinguish between liturgy and Scripture.'

Time passed by. Twenty years, in fact. Then a series of heartbreaking circumstances at church led to her studying for the Bishop's Certificate (learning how the Anglican Church 'ticks').

One assignment determined that she attend a different church and write a critical essay about it. 'The church chosen was Ebenezer Church, Mold, Baptist by denomination and evangelical. Having been convent-trained it was the last place

I would have expected to be. To say that I was amazed at the difference is putting it mildly.'

The first person this high Anglican met was the then secretary to the Bishop of Chester. 'So that was OK, I wasn't really betraying the *alma* mater if someone who mixed with Anglicans was there.'

As well as her other studies, she was also learning a different language – British Sign Language. A friend, Muriel invited Carolyn to attend a Christian sign language class. It was there that they also focused on the Lord Jesus and the Word of God, the Bible.

'All this truth I was at last hearing. When studying Peter's declaration of Jesus as Messiah (Mark 8:29), Muriel saw the look on my face and my corrugated brow and asked what the problem was. 'Peter was the first pope, wasn't he?' I blurted out. At that moment I realized that, although I was learning to communicate with deaf people, I was the one who had been deaf all through my life, and that, as the Bible puts it, there is 'one mediator between God and men, the man Christ Jesus' (1 Tim. 2:5).

At 58 years of age, Carolyn opened the Bible properly that evening for the first time. Her phone bill to Muriel increased dramatically as she asked question after question, sometimes late into the night. Muriel was very patient. 'I just couldn't get enough of the Bible,' Carolyn remembers. Later Muriel invited her to Keswick, where every year a Christian convention is held in the town. Here Carolyn was able to be among thousands of people who had come to a living personal faith in Jesus Christ.

Carolyn explains what or who has made the difference in her

life. 'The Lord Jesus Christ has died for me personally on that cross in tremendous pain. Why? Because of the enormity of my sin. The very least I can do is be sorry for all the ways I offend Him and to resolve to turn away from sin and ask Him to be Lord of my life. He is my Saviour who has reconciled me to God. Although the first time of doing this is the key to opening the door, it is continual. While elated at finally knowing this, I was also overwhelmed. There was the sense of guilt that my sin had put Him there, the awe and yet thankfulness that Jesus would bother to do this for me – I had messed Him about through my life – and understanding that His saving was not anything of my own doing or efforts. I prayed from the heart to Jesus.'

Carolyn returned from Keswick knowing that she must act and respond to God's will. Her own Anglican church was becoming rather liberal in its beliefs, she felt. Having been invited to become further involved with the church in Wales, Carolyn decided, after prayer, reading the Bible and seeking advice, that it was not God's will for her to pursue any position within its ranks.

In 2004 Muriel was signing for the deaf at a special service at Ebenezer Church in Mold. Carolyn was being baptized as an adult by immersion in water to signify that her old life was buried and that she had new life in Christ.

'The Lord has waited to be gracious to me … at 61 years old. So what of the music that used to dominate everything? I am privileged to play along with many instrumentalists, and to contribute to church worship, continuing to teach and be an accompanist.'

Her enthusiasm for Christ knows no bounds!

*I waited for the L*ORD*; he turned to me and heard my cry.*
He lifted me out of the slimy pit, out of the mud and mire;
he set my feet on a rock and gave me a firm place to stand.
He put a new song in my mouth, a hymn of praise to our God.
*Many will see and fear and put their trust in the L*ORD*.*

(Ps. 40:1–3)

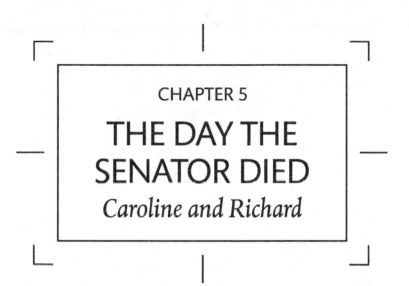

CHAPTER 5

THE DAY THE SENATOR DIED
Caroline and Richard

When something significant happens in world history, such as a natural disaster, the outbreak of war, or the death of a famous person, the event may cause us to stop what we are doing and ponder its enormity, and the seriousness of its effect.

When Robert Kennedy, the younger brother of the late President John F. Kennedy, entered the Ambassador Hotel in Los Angeles on a June day in 1968, he knew that he was going to attend a press conference as part of the celebration of his recent political victory. What he didn't know was that Sirhan Sirhan was there to assassinate him. Shots rang out. The senator was rushed to the Good Samaritan Hospital where, despite surgery, he died the next day from his injuries. News spread around the world. Another of America's Kennedy clan had been assassinated in public.

Caroline, who was 18 years old, was alone in her bedroom in England. It was late at night. She was stunned, as was everyone else on hearing the tragic news.

> **" What happened next Caroline finds hard to explain. It was not visual, nor did anything physical or strange happen around her. But it was definitely more than a mere thought... "**

'I remember asking out loud in the empty room why good people were constantly thwarted or killed in their attempts to do good. I thought back over history; over all the countless people who had died for their country or for a good cause. Why?'

What happened next Caroline finds hard to explain. It was not visual, nor did anything physical or strange happen around her. But it was definitely more than a mere thought ...

'It definitely came from "without", and I felt overwhelmed with this comforting certainty that I needed to have faith. "Faith in what?" you might ask. In my certainty I knew the faith I needed was faith in God. This experience was quite vague, since it did not give me much idea who God was. However, it was to be a milestone, because this certainty prompted me to take seriously and investigate from then on anything Christian that came my way.'

Anyone born in the middle of the twentieth century in the UK, when asked what religion they were, would probably have said 'Christian'. What they meant by that, of course, could be any number of things, including just the fact of being born in a nominal Christian country. The statement would be made regardless of denomination or frequency of attendance at church or chapel. However, there was a general belief in the Christian's God, the Triune God who is One – Father, Son and Holy Spirit. Many children at some time had attended Sunday school, and at school had a daily time of worship.

Caroline was born into a family in a village in the south of England. Some of her earliest memories are of breathtakingly beautiful countryside and of sitting with her parents and friends on summer Sunday mornings in the comfort of their English garden full of scented flowers listening to the hum of bumblebees.

'My family did not often go to church, but I did know about God. My father would tell me about Adam and Eve and Satan, describing him with the same zest given to picturing wicked witches in fairy stories, and made me giggle.'

She was told about the need to be good and that only good people go to heaven. The former is true but the latter, according to the Bible, is not. The notion was generally held that it was important to know about religion and the stories in the Bible, but not to take them too seriously. It was a respectable thing to do. But Caroline did, on occasions, go to church.

'Our beautiful village had an equally beautiful Norman church in its midst. I remember standing on the wooden pew so that I could sing the hymns with my parents. Afterwards, as a rare treat, we would call in at the paper shop to buy a bar of chocolate, which we shared, having a few squares each.

The vicar wore glasses and used to dress in a black cassock.' He made a lasting impression on Caroline who, as a young

" I remember standing on the wooden pew so that I could sing the hymns with my parents. Afterwards, as a rare treat, we would call in at the paper shop to buy a bar of chocolate, which we shared, having a few squares each."

child, thought he was God! There was a moment when her father and the vicar both started to speak at once to each other. Caroline stiffened and said in no uncertain terms: 'Ssh, Daddy, God's talking!'

From her halcyon days Caroline has fleeting memories of a serialized television production called *Jesus of Nazareth*. What stuck in her mind was that Jesus was portrayed as very kind and trustworthy, but also capable of anger as he turned over the tables in the Temple. Privately, she remembered the portrayal of the crowd being nasty to Him and how indignant she felt about it all.

The next vicar who took over at the church was considered by villagers as being too conversational with God.

'Looking back, what I learned from him that was helpful was that God was someone I could have a relationship with, and talk to in an informal way. My main contact with him was mainly through school, where he gave Scripture lessons. But part of me remained sceptical in the same way that I was sceptical of conjurors and their magical tricks.'

Her parents saw that she was becoming quite a fearful child who needed an encouraging and loving environment, so Caroline's senior school was chosen with that in mind. Caroline was happy there. It was nominally a Christian school where, although she did not understand it, she became well versed in the main Bible stories, and learned by heart many of the sound prayers from *The Book of Common Prayer*.

'My mother had suffered hugely in various ways. She told me that there had been a couple of crises since she had become a wife and a mother. Things for the family were so difficult that she could not see a way forward, and she had no idea what to do. She told me that she had felt that she had no other option but to offer it all up to God and say, "I have no idea what to do. I have no option but to leave it up to You." Each

> **" She was quite certain that she had fallen upon a religious truth."**

time she was brought to this point, something materialized quite soon to alleviate the situation. She was quite certain that she had fallen upon a religious truth.'

So when Robert Kennedy died, Caroline had some certainty of faith, but she also had mixed religious ideas. She had no real knowledge or relationship with God until later on during her working life, when she came across a group of Christians who ran a weekly Bible study, which she joined. Although what she heard there made an impression on her (particularly the point that Jesus died so that our sins could be forgiven) she could not see the significance of eternal life.

'I could only see the point of Christianity inasmuch as it applied to life on this earth. In addition, I felt quite isolated in this group I did not feel I was developing real friendships with any of them. After a while I left.'

Life moved on, and before long Caroline met and married her husband, settling down to a happy life.

'My husband was not a believer in God. Like me, he believed the ultimate was to do good in this world without thinking about the next, and together we aspired to this. It seemed easier to play down any remaining questions I had. I became what I described inwardly to myself as "a Christian fence-sitter"; something that deep down I did not feel proud of because it felt like a cop-out.

I remember feeling that atheists had a greater respect for God than I did as a fence-sitter.

'We went on to have two lovely sons, and I was keen for them to have access to learning about God. That certainty of God's existence that I gained all those years ago had never left me, and I wanted them to be able to capture what I had of this. But I was also concerned that the boys should not be frightened as I had been. So, when they asked me about God, I always told them I believed in Him, but I did not say very much more for fear of doing more harm than good. Eventually the time came when, as a teenager, our elder son attended confirmation classes at school. I remember being surprised that my son never seemed to open his Bible; after all, isn't that what confirmation classes are for?

'I decided to talk to him about it. I asked him if they had mentioned why Jesus had died. "No! What do you mean?" he asked in amazement. I told him that I knew Jesus' death was something to do with forgiving our sins, and I mentioned my concern that there seemed to be no reference to the Bible in his confirmation classes. My husband and I persuaded him not to go ahead with being confirmed at this stage, as we both recognized that this was not something to undertake with only a superficial understanding of what it was about.'

" Heaven is not a reward for doing good, but a gift. Nothing we can do could ever get us to God. "

Shortly after this, her son went along with some friends to a youth group at a local church where for the first time he learned about the gospel, the good news of Jesus Christ. The reason why Jesus died on the cross was to be as a substitute for us, a Saviour. He took on Himself the punishment for our sin; punishment which we deserve because we all have fallen short of God's standard, which cannot be ignored. Jesus then rose from the dead to make a way for us to be with Him forever. Heaven is not a reward for doing good, but a gift. Nothing we can do could ever get us to God. God Himself provided the only way through His Son, who is the way, the truth and the life; the only mediator between God and humanity.

Caroline's son made a connection between what he was hearing and what his mother had been trying to tell him. Shortly afterwards, he became a Christian – not just nominally, or by going to church, but by trusting in and believing in the finished work of Christ as the only means of salvation from sin. He not only believed in Jesus Christ but also now had a new, personal, living relationship with Him, which was transforming his life. Not long after, his brother also became a Christian.

A few months later it was Christmas, one of the busiest times in the church calendar, when parents and grandparents attend seasonal services. Caroline went along to a carol service at her sons' church. In his sermon, the vicar clearly spelt out the marks of a true Christian. Caroline came home feeling much better. 'I was now no longer a shameful fence-sitter. I now knew that I was definitely *not* a Christian.'

> **" I was now no longer a shameful fence-sitter. I now knew that I was definitely not a Christian."**

Caroline found some strange comfort in that, but it didn't last long. Half-heartedly one day she agreed to read a verse from the Bible that her son wanted to show her. 'Do not be anxious about anything, but in everything, by prayer and petition, with thanksgiving, present your requests to God' (Phil. 4:6).

'This struck a chord with me. I clearly was not feeling as much at peace as I thought. At our boys' bidding, we started attending their church more regularly.

'Over the next few weeks I became conscious of depressing news headlines which seemed to reflect a general apathy about life; the breaking down of family life and society, the rise of violence in the home and on the streets, not to mention wars and political uprisings throughout the world. I became weighed down by a sense of joylessness in the world, and also in myself. One day, I found myself getting cross about something and realized that God deserved better than this from me. I began praying: "I cannot carry on sitting on the fence any more. If You are who You say You are, You will know what to do to help me with this."'

Among the many Christmas cards received was one some friends had sent which contained an extract from Matthew's Gospel. It concerned the issue of eternal life.

'I came to understand that my becoming a Christian concerned not only me but also God. I became aware of how much bigger God is than this world and everything in it. It gave me hope. Shortly afterwards I became a real Christian.'

> **" I became aware of how much bigger God is than this world and everything in it. It gave me hope. "**

Caroline's experience years ago at the time of the death of Senator Edward Kennedy, the memories of *Jesus of Nazareth*, as well as various incidents, all helped in God's plan to guide her to personal faith in Him.

'One concern that I had was that my

husband, Richard, did not believe,' she says. 'I had heard stories of this kind of thing coming between couples, and it worried me. I prayed about it and talked to my husband. I asked him if he would come to church with me so that even if he did not believe, he could get some idea of what I had committed myself to. I stressed to him that I was not putting him under pressure to become a Christian, to which he replied very reassuringly, "No, I know you never would." He said he was very happy to come with me on that basis.'

Richard's family background was that of the army, his officer father having been born in India and his grandfather having served in the Indian army at the time of the Raj. Consequently, in his early life, Richard moved houses a few times, following his father's postings. At the age of 8 he was sent to a boarding preparatory school, which was excellent and an enjoyable experience. Although not a games player, he did well academically. Traditionally these schools often had a chapel and quite an emphasis on divinity and 'church Christianity' within the curriculum. His senior public school years followed a similar pattern, particularly as the headmaster was an ordained minister in the Church of England. Richard explains what effect, if any, good or bad, all this religion had on his life:

'I was interested enough to be confirmed and regularly attend church while at school, but despite this upbringing steeped in church traditions I did not understand the true message of the gospel. Having left school I went up to university where almost immediately my churchgoing ceased. There was an active Christian Union, but they were regarded as an eccentric clique by the majority of the students, being referred to as the "God Squad".

'After university, I started employment as an electronic engineer in a large industrial company. This I also enjoyed, gaining much fulfilment and satisfaction in my work. Marriage followed, with both my wife and I taking our wedding vows seriously, but not seeing them in a particularly Christian context. We believed we led good lives, and brought up our sons with Christian values, but in fact we were not true Christian believers. For my own part, I have to admit that I did nothing to encourage our boys in any Christian belief.'

When his boys voluntarily started attending a local church youth group, Richard was quite pleased as it was well run and kept youngsters off the streets. But after their decisions to commit themselves wholeheartedly to Christ as their Lord and Saviour, Richard had a few reservations.

'I was not sure initially what to make of it. But I was reassured after meeting the youth leaders, whom I liked. Soon after, the boys invited my wife and me to attend the church Christmas carol service, which was a wonderful occasion, with candles, traditional carols and a great choir. Then came the sermon. I cannot remember what it was about, but I do remember the gospel message being explained in a way I had never heard before. What was more, the preacher did not ask us to take his word for it, but he explained that everything he was telling us was written in the Bible, where we could check it for ourselves. This was preaching that appealed to my intellectual approach to life, but nevertheless I was still very sceptical.

'At this time I was about 50 years old. In common with most people of this age I had become quite set in my views, and I was a determined agnostic. It was hard at such a time of life to admit I might have been mistaken in my beliefs all those years.'

By now his wife had also become a committed Christian, as well as his boys. Richard was much more uncertain, but agreed to support her and go with her to church, where he heard regular expository preaching which he found quite attractive. He also started reading books such as Frank Morison's *Who Moved the Stone?* and *Knowing God* by Jim Packer. At church they joined a *Christianity Explored* group, followed by another course called *Discipleship Explored.*

'These excellent courses led by staff from the church, combined with the Sunday preaching and reading Christian books, finally convinced me that the life I had been living was not complete. I had a loving wife, two successful children and a successful career – who could want more? However, I realized that I was still searching for a real meaning to life. At work I had seen many highly successful professional men retire and then be mainly forgotten by their colleagues. For many, their professional achievements amounted to very little when they were no longer working. When they died, their work was quickly forgotten. The Christian message of justification by faith through God's grace and the atoning sacrifice of His Son Jesus Christ was truly life-changing. What is more, I did not have to take some church minister's word for it, I could see it written down in the Bible, with the Old Testament prophecies and eyewitness accounts of the New Testament.'

Becoming a Christian later in life can be a challenge. Richard and Caroline value the help they receive from friends, and the solid support group they have at their church.

CHAPTER 6

THE TUPPERWARE MAN

Barrie Bailey

Boxes of different sizes and shapes have always figured prominently in Barrie's life.

His first encounter with a box was when he was born. The hospital in Farnborough, Kent had run out of cots on that memorable day in December during the Second World War. The only thing available was a wooden drawer. Wartime meant that life was hard, frugal and dangerous. The Bailey family lived in Bromley, which was close to London. Therefore during the Blitz they experienced some risky times. During an air raid, Barrie would be placed in the cupboard under the stairs with their greyhound, Bess, who would stand over him to protect him.

Barrie's father had managed a fruit and vegetable shop in peace time, but throughout the war he was a fireman with the London Fire Brigade. Barrie's mother did fire-watching duties. They were a very hard-working couple who set a good example to Barrie.

'At the end of the war, we moved to Slough. Dad worked at the Mars factory for a few years before once again returning to the greengrocery trade, which he so loved, again as a manager of a shop. During the school holidays, I would go with my father to Brentford wholesale fruit and vegetable market.

By 1948, my parents had bought a caravan, which was kept on a farm at Pagham close to Bognor Regis. My father did not keep good health, and I have memories of milk puddings and fish being cooked for him, while other food was prepared for me.

'In the early fifties, my father was horrified to see the price of Jersey potatoes in the shop at the caravan site. This prompted my parents to look for their own premises in Pagham so that they could trade as greengrocers there. With much hard work, they managed to still run the shop in Slough as well as the new one. Dad would drive down with new stock each night, stay over and then go back to Slough in the early morning. Inevitably this led to my father collapsing with a perforated ulcer needing an operation in hospital.'

Barrie's mother took over the business responsibilities, which meant that now she had to rely on local wholesalers instead of direct purchases from the market. Although Barrie was only 11 at that time, he too had to play his part and have some responsibilities. It was all good experience, which he would need in later years. Having recovered from his operation, Barrie's father decided to sell the house in Slough and buy one in Pagham.

School runs by mums in 4x4s were not the norm for schoolchildren in those days. To get to school Barrie had two bus journeys, but mostly children walked. Before school he had to complete a long paper round, and at weekends and holidays had to help in the shop.

" *I could not wait to leave school. I just wanted to be a greengrocer, so I did not need education for that.* "

'I could not wait to leave school. I just wanted to be a greengrocer, so I did not need education for that. I left school when I was 15 years and ten days old. It was great and I had a job. What more could I want? I worked for my parents and for an electrician friend who also did painting and decorating.'

Religion? This did not really figure in Barrie's life, although he was a choirboy at St Thomas à Becket church in Pagham. He had been a war baby so had not been christened. He had decided to be confirmed when he was 13 and, in order for that to happen, he had to be baptized, which was quite brave for a lad his age.

Hard work and enthusiasm became hallmarks of his life, encouraged also by others and their example. From practical experience, he was aware that this could pay off in time. His parents were able to buy a fifteenth-century thatched cottage, complete with a beam marked 1402, from a woman who had seen their hard work. She was so impressed that she dropped the asking price. The cottage was just behind the shop.

" *By now, any attendance at church had long been discarded.* "

By now, any attendance at church had long been discarded. The business was thriving, so Barrie was given more and more responsibility.

The next decade saw him achieving an ambition to become a wholesale fruit and vegetable salesman. A friend he had helped in the past offered him a position as driver/salesman. Barrie had gained much from his father's expertise with display and purchase of fruit and vegetables. His mother's influence was in showing him the importance of bookkeeping and in protecting hard-earned money. His other love was lorries.

Early starts were always the order of the day for drivers. Usually, it was 5.30 a.m., but if he went to Borough Market, in the heart of London, then he had to leave at 4 a.m. Barrie thought it was a great life, thoroughly enjoying every minute of it, until the boss overheard something he said.

> **" I took umbrage and left, went home and told my parents that I was going to start my own business. "**

'I mentioned that I was thinking of changing my van for a Morris 1000 Traveller. The boss challenged me as to how I could afford this, as my wages were £10 per week with one old penny per pound commission! I took umbrage and left, went home and told my parents that I was going to start my own business.'

Not yet 21, Barrie soon built up a customer base in and around the area. He needed a loan to purchase a new lorry but within four years this was paid off.

Other things were 'paying off', too, but this time in the world of romance. A couple in Bognor had a daughter, Liz, who was studying music at Cardiff University. Barrie used to make deliveries to her parents' shop. Before long they were 'an item', then engaged. Marriage followed in 1966 in a registry office. Liz had a Christian background, so she found the choice of venue a bit hard, but Barrie had no idea what it meant to be a Christian.

His parents could not attend the wedding as it was on a Saturday, the busiest trading day. But they gave the newlyweds a little bungalow in which they were really happy.

The following years were busy, as not only were business ventures thriving (including an ice cream stall), but also the family was growing. Claire, John and James arrived on the scene, but sadly Barrie's father passed away. With more work to do, especially as his mother's health failed, there was little time for holidays – just four days.

Some changes were ahead when Barrie and Liz started attending Clymping Church, which Liz had attended in the past. A bigger house was needed, and Barrie decided it was time to sell the business. First he was a milkman, and then he moved to the Geest organization as a branch director at the wholesale market. There were 2 a.m. starts this time, but it meant that he was home in the afternoons and, of course, weekends. And at last, there were holidays.

After years of dealing with boxes of fruit and veg, eventually an opportunity arose to make some money out of selling boxes themselves – Tupperware boxes.

In 1937, Earl Silas Tupper was a chemist and employee at a Du Pont chemical plant. Mr Tupper needed plastic for his experiments, but in those early days it was not a very good product. Du Pont arranged to sell him remnants in the form of polythene slag, which was hard, smelly and almost impossible to work with. Mr Tupper was able to purify it, turning it into a mouldable plastic. This had never been done before. The box or bowl could now be made, but what about the lid? The inspiration for the famous seal came from a lid on a tin of paint, as this was able to keep the paint from drying out for years. Mr Tupper wanted a plastic container with a lid that was watertight, kept food fresh and was spill-proof. Tupperware was born.

Tupper had the invention but did not know how to market it. Enter Brownie Wise. She was given some bowls, but took three days to figure out how the seal worked. She was so excited with these new tubs that she wanted to tell all her friends. Thus the Party Plan method of selling was invented, and used for selling the now famous Tupperware.

In 1977, Liz hosted a Tupperware party in their home, and decided she would like to become a Tupperware demonstrator. They never dreamt how this would affect their future or where it would lead.

Barrie explains: 'Before long, she was invited to become a manager. By the eighties we decided to move nearer to Brighton as that was where I worked, and the local Tupperware distributors were also based there. I was supportive of Liz, but I did not realize the potential of what she was doing until I attended some national meetings. I also noted the lifestyle of the distributors who supplied Liz. In fact they were able to use my services to do some deliveries for them. I saw their business more closely and I liked what I saw.

In Tupperware there were many exciting promotions that could be achieved. Liz had won her way to a weekend at the Royal Garden Hotel in Kensington. During this weekend, I became aware for the first time that Liz was among the very top managers in the UK and Ireland and her peers were amazed that she was not going on the forthcoming trip to the USA. After that weekend, I asked her what she needed to do. When she told me, I decided that I was going to help her in any way I could to achieve the next such trip. I had not bargained for it being Egypt! Liz was amongst the top three managers nationally, achieving the trip in just eight months rather than twelve.'

> " *Liz was amongst the top three managers nationally, achieving the trip in just eight months rather than twelve.*"

Up until then, Barrie's life was pretty much like that of his contemporaries. He had worked hard to provide a decent living and home for his wife and family, but God just didn't figure in it at all.

Liz's success resulted in them being given the opportunity to become distributors themselves, working together in Exeter. Although it was hard to uproot the family, they decided to go, and loved it right from the start. It was very much like going home for Liz, as she had family nearby.

'We each had a distinct role to play in this partnership. Liz had a motivational role. It fulfilled her interest in people and what made them tick. My role was logistical in ensuring the efficient running of the warehouse and all matters of stock control, together with deliveries.' They truly were an ideal team.

'In Exeter, we had another top manager within our distributorship. She and her husband were great friends to us, supporting us in so many ways, not just within the business. They attended St Thomas Baptist Church not just on a Sunday, but were fully involved on the diaconate and over 18's group. The distributors we knew who lived in Taunton were Christians as well, and also attended a Baptist church. When

> **" When we arrived at Exeter we had not planned that church would be on the agenda! "**

I took deliveries there, I would be invited in for a cup of tea, and I would notice the Bible out on the kitchen table. Apart from the conversations about the business, we inevitably used to talk about their activities at church. When we arrived at Exeter we had not planned that church would be on the agenda!

'Over those years, I was unaware that people were praying for me.

In 1985, when we were experiencing a particularly difficult time with our daughter, Liz felt compelled to attend church one Sunday morning. She experienced a real sense of homecoming, and her faith in her Saviour was renewed. As I always supported Liz in anything she did, when she decided to be baptized I agreed to attend. I had never seen a baptism by immersion before in my life. I certainly had no plan to follow her.'

However, Barrie did begin to attend church in the evenings fairly regularly. He had never heard someone preaching about the Bible in such a detailed way, and making it come alive. The people really made him feel welcome.

Having support from the church fellowship meant a lot to Barrie, especially when their first grandchild died tragically at just nine weeks old.

'Witnessing paramedics endeavouring to resuscitate this tiny child was horrendous, and having to support my daughter was heartbreaking. The experience was even more traumatic as the baby's father was in prison. The pastor visited us and took the funeral, which was difficult because of the need for the father to be handcuffed to the wardens.

'The help from the church fellowship was amazing. I, as always, wanted to be in control. But I will never forget what the pastor said: "Let the police police, the undertaker undertake and the minister minister." It was a very tense time that had a profound effect on the family and me. Suddenly all the ambitions and expectations that everyone had for this little life were all useless.'

" Witnessing paramedics endeavouring to resuscitate this tiny child was horrendous, and having to support my daughter was heartbreaking."

Barrie's own health was affected by stress and grief over the next few years. Also an infection didn't help as he went into a bout of depression for a couple of weeks.

Then, at church, the minister asked when had he received Jesus into his life?

'I found that I could not give him an answer. He loaned me a book about the life of Hudson Taylor, who was a famous Yorkshire missionary to China in the nineteenth century. Once I had finished it, the minister came to see me at home. He explained to me how Jesus had died for me personally and I received Jesus as my Saviour on 2 January 1992. What a way to start a new year! 'I thought that sin was centred on the Ten Commandments. I didn't realize that aggressive behaviour, wrong words being said, and general thoughtlessness were all sins. I attended classes a little later before I was baptized to declare my new faith in God publicly and identify with the truth that Jesus has died and risen again. I felt that a load had been lifted from me and so began my new relationship with Jesus Christ.

> **" I realize that all the time God was in control, working out His purpose for me. He was there in all the steps along the way. The only problem was that I did not know it. God's timing is perfect. "**

'I realize that all the time God was in control, working out His purpose for me. He was there in all the steps along the way. The only problem was that I did not know it. God's timing is perfect.'

The business flourished with more responsibilities being taken on. Life was not without its problems, but Barrie was not going through them alone. With faith in God and through prayer and reading the Bible, he was able to make decisions and choices in a different light. Eventually, Liz retired to give more time to the family. Barrie carried on and for a while was in charge of the national distribution of Tupperware. When the company decided to close the business in the UK and Ireland, he too retired.

'When I was younger, my ambition was to earn enough money to retire at 30 and drive around in a Triumph 2000! I would never have believed that for me to become a Christian was to have a change of attitude to my whole life. My life experiences are still important, and now I can see how the Lord uses them for His purposes. These days, my assurance is in the risen Jesus Christ and what my future holds with Him.'

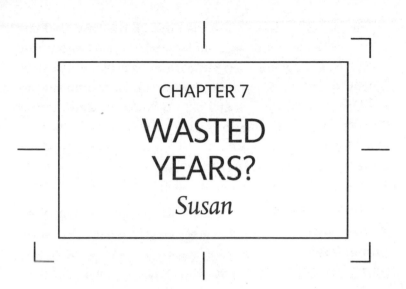

CHAPTER 7
WASTED YEARS?
Susan

'I was born in the city of Dublin,' says Susan. 'I am a twin. When we reached 2 years of age, our mother decided that she could no longer deal with us. We were put into a children's home where I was to remain for the next sixteen years.

'Although it was a religious home, as in many other institutions, life was tough. Mental, physical and sexual abuse was common. Despite a large number of children in the home, it could be a very lonely place; a place where you seemed to be constantly in trouble.

'Every morning after breakfast and again after dinner we were read to from the Bible. It was through these Bible stories that I used to hear of this wonderful person who loved and cared for people, even children. Having never really been shown any love or affection, I yearned for this feeling of being wanted. This person they read about in the Bible never seemed to be in a bad mood or angry, but was always caring, gentle and loving.

'One day, when I was about 8 years old, I was accused of doing something I had not done. And "stubborn" being my middle name, I was not going to give in and say I was guilty – this was usually the best tactic, because you were punished immediately and that was the end of the matter. So I was made to stay indoors, which was extremely hard for me, being a tomboy. I was confined to my room until such a time as I was ready to confess. After a couple of days, an adult came into the room and told me to go out with all the other children and play.

> **" I ran outside immediately and sat down on a bench. My emotions were all over the place. "**

'I ran outside immediately and sat down on a bench. My emotions were all over the place. One second I was very angry, then the next second happy, then sad. Who were these people that could do this to me? No "sorry", no explanation as to why they had come to the conclusion that I was no longer guilty. Tears welled up in my eyes and I squeezed them tightly shut so as not to let any teardrops fall, as I had learned from an early age not to let emotions show. I was feeling so down, so alone, so empty, but longing for something – what?

'Then these words came into my head from a song we sometimes sang:

What a friend we have in Jesus,
All our sins and griefs to bear!
What a privilege to carry
everything to God in prayer!
*...take it to the Lord in prayer.**

So as I sat on this bench, I asked Jesus if He would be my friend.'

Susan finds it hard to find words to describe how she immediately knew that her prayer had been answered. An almost tangible feeling overwhelmed her, bringing peace and assurance of being a friend of God.

When Susan reached her teenage years, things became really tough. 'Being the "smart boots" I thought I was, knowing everything, as teens do, I felt I didn't need Jesus any more. So I turned my back on Him and mixed with the wrong people ... married the wrong man ... and wasted many years trying to do my own thing, which now I deeply regret. Take my advice – don't do as I did, because it is not worth it. The grass is not greener on the other side. I know. I've been there.'

A few years ago, after her children had left home, Susan downsized to a small flat in Kingston upon Thames. At first she found the new-found freedom and time bliss, but there was still a void in her life. That 'inner voice' that she had heard calling her over the years was even more prominent. However, she tried to push it away, busying herself with various charitable works, which were very worthy causes but didn't satisfy.

Another distraction was a new man in her life. Their evenings were very merry, eating and drinking with a new set of friends. It didn't take long for Susan to realize that she could dull the emptiness and push away demons that troubled her by drinking alcohol. Very soon it was the norm, and something upon which she relied heavily.

" It didn't take long for Susan to realize that she could dull the emptiness and push away demons that troubled her by drinking alcohol."

One afternoon, her granddaughter, then aged 3, visited her unexpectedly. Susan greeted her with a kiss as she normally would. 'Ugh, Nanny,' the child cried. 'You smell of beer!'

'I was so ashamed,' says Susan. 'I was so glad no one heard her. But, can you believe it, my response was to drink some more. I was trying to dull my embarrassment, drinking on my own and not just when out with friends.'

Somehow Susan still managed to keep working, until one Monday when she realized she had overdone it after a weekend of socializing and heavy drinking. Shaking, feeling sick and very frightened, Susan telephoned her daughter.

> **" I knew that I had gone too far this time. "**

'I knew that I had gone too far this time. I saw a doctor the same day and was diagnosed with alcohol poisoning. I was warned that I must stop drinking, and was even advised to go away to a clinic for three weeks. It could be arranged that very day. I was shocked. I couldn't do that. Everyone would know that I had a drink problem, which up until then I had kept secret.'

Susan did stop drinking, but before long a feeling engulfed her that she describes as 'a dark, black blanket'. It made her wish she could 'end it all'. Maybe it would be for the best? Her heart was breaking. She felt she just could not take any more. Tears began to flow until there was anguished sobbing. It was then that she thought of God. It was as though He was calling her to Himself.

'I crumpled to the floor and begged Jesus to forgive me for the hurt I had caused Him, and the years I had wasted. From that moment on I decided I would follow Him and go His way. I told God that I would need His help, as I needed to end an unhealthy relationship with a man. I needed help to turn my life around. I wanted a life that God would be pleased with.'

Susan knew she needed to find a church where she could not only worship God, but also socialize and talk with other Christians. But how do you find a 'good' church, one that believes and teaches the Bible and preaches the gospel, the good news of Jesus Christ? Eventually, she looked in the Yellow Pages, where she came across Hook Evangelical Church, near Kingston upon Thames. There was no answer on the phone number given, but being persistent in her enquiries, she tried the Thompson directory too. There, to her delight, was a large advert for that same church, but also giving the times of the services. 'I was so pleased that I thanked God there and then. The very next Sunday I went along to the service and have continued since.'

Going to church didn't make Susan a Christian, but it was a place where she could learn more about God and worship Him with others who also had put their trust in Him. Susan had become very much aware of her own sin, was sorry, and wanted to turn from it. She realized again the truth that Jesus suffered and died, taking the punishment that she deserved, but through His resurrection He is able to give new, eternal, life. She believed and put her trust in Him. It wasn't about Susan 'turning over a new leaf'. It wasn't all about trying. It was about trusting in and experiencing God, who had given her new life based on mercy and forgiveness.

Susan now has a reason for living and a purpose for going on. She keeps in touch with her twin sister, and continues to play an active role in the life of her church.

* 'What a Friend We Have in Jesus', Joseph Scriven, 1820–1886.

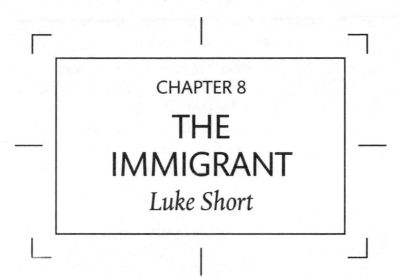

CHAPTER 8
THE IMMIGRANT
Luke Short

To leave your country to start a new life in a place where you are considered a foreigner must be daunting, yet exciting. In the new country, immigrants are greeted and treated with a variety of responses – suspicion, fear, animosity, resentment, or with genuine hospitality, generosity and encouragement.

The flow of people from place to place is not just a new phenomenon, but has been around for thousands of years.

Luke Short was an immigrant. Very little is known of him. Who his family were, his trade, where he settled and what he accomplished have not been written down in detail. As far as history is concerned, he was insignificant to the world, but not to God.

We would not have even known his name had it not been for Robert Murray McCheyne, a famous nineteenth-century Christian preacher from Dundee in Scotland, who has left us with the only remaining nugget of intriguing information about this 15-year-old American immigrant.

In the jigsaw of this life, one important piece was a man called John Flavell who was born in the seventeenth century in Bromsgrove, Worcestershire. His father had been a minister but died of the plague in 1665 while in prison for non-conformity (he was a Protestant, but not an Anglican). John, obviously undeterred by the hazards of the job, also became a minister. Some men did go into this line of work because it was expected of them, but some were genuine in their belief that they were called of God to be pastors and preachers of the Bible. The non-conformists in particular attracted opposition. The Puritans, so called because of their attitude to the behaviour of that period, had a significant influence on society and the history of religion.

In the language of that time, one of John Flavell's parishioners in Dartmouth wrote of him:

I could say much, though not enough of the excellency of his preaching; of his seasonable, suitable, and spiritual matter; of his plain expositions of Scripture; his talking method, his genuine and natural deductions, his convincing arguments, his clear and powerful demonstrations, his heart-searching applications, and his comfortable supports to those that were afflicted in conscience. In short, that person must have a very soft head, or a very hard heart, or both, that could sit under his ministry unaffected.*

The writings of John Flavell are still in print and are published by the Banner of Truth Trust.

Luke Short was only young when he listened to John Flavell

preach back in England. The Bible text that was being preached on was 'If any man love not the Lord Jesus Christ, let him be Anathema' (1 Cor. 16:22, KJV). We have no record of what Luke Short thought when he first heard the sermon but, amazingly, 85 years later, while working in the fields, he suddenly remembered the sermon where Flavell preached on the horror of dying under God's curse. God so spoke to his inner conscience that even at such a great age he called out to God for mercy and to save him from his sins.

According to the records of First Congregational Church of Middleborough, Massachusetts, USA (founded by the sons of the Pilgrim Fathers in 1629), Luke Short worshipped there 'joining the church when he was over 100 and living to the ripe old age of 116. He was present at the beheading of King Charles the First in 1649, and he had seen Oliver Cromwell.

Whilst we can all give our date of birth, none of us knows the time or day when we will breathe our last. But the Bible says, 'Everyone who calls on the name of the Lord will be saved' (Rom. 10:13).

Luke Short, while an immigrant on this earth, trusted in the one true God before he made his final journey to become a citizen of heaven for eternity.

* Erasmus Middleton, *Evangelical Biography*, 4:50–51.

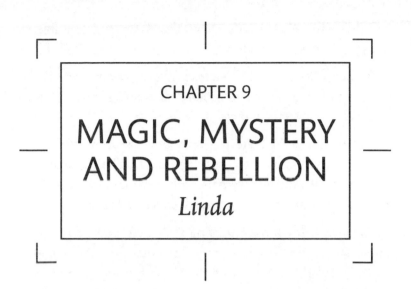

CHAPTER 9

MAGIC, MYSTERY AND REBELLION

Linda

'When I first came into the world, my mother used to say that the only thing that was white in my pram was a circle on the pillow where my head had been. Everything else, including me, was covered in coal dust from the mines of the small Yorkshire town where I spent the first part of my life. However, I survived, and with my lungs intact.'

Linda's background had 'respectability' written all over it. There was a strong sense of family duty as she grew up, with no hint of the rebellion ahead. Her father was a Methodist minister. She was happy to conform, and went to church, adopting family attitudes and expectations.

'I joined with my peer group in being received into membership of the Methodist Church. I can remember how magical and mysterious it felt to be officially recognized – although at the age of 13 I do wonder how much that was due to a continuing sense of conformity. One of my expectations –

and also of that era – was that it was necessary, and desirable, to marry, and have 2.4 children.'

Married at the age of 21 to a man from a very different social background, Linda decided to enrol at a college in London to study Occupational Therapy.

'We moved to facilitate my travelling which uprooted my husband from familiar territory and necessitated a change of job. My studies and involvement with student life took me on a new exciting path, but the marriage ended after four years.

'The people I was now meeting with were politically active, interested in philosophy, mysticism and the arts. I joined "bedsitter world" where I met my second husband. His was a world dedicated to expanding the mind and the senses. There were drug-induced experiences, and exploration of Eastern philosophies, art and music. We joined the hippie exodus from the cities in the early seventies and moved to a derelict cottage in mid Wales. There was no electricity, no water or road access.

'It was both exciting and rewarding to be part of a movement of young people out to change the world by seeking an alternative to the consumer society. We wanted to live a simpler, cleaner and better life. Vegetables were home grown. Traditional ways of doing things were tried. It sounds idyllic, but the marriage was not a happy one. I became increasingly concerned for our two children, who were growing up in an atmosphere of disharmony, disrespect and lack of trust.'

Eventually, with a baby and a 5-year-old, Linda left the 'dream-life in the back of beyond' to move to a council estate in a local market town. She was on her own raising the children, but had the support of some friends and a good local school. However, she was still exploring various religious and philosophical ideas, while relying on things such as astrology and forms of divination for guidance.

'Many so-called New Age ideas reinforced my belief that we are all responsible for our actions, and will attract to ourselves what we need for our learning. Actually, I learned many life skills and survival techniques that have stood the test of time. But the central belief I had then was that we are, each one, at the centre of our own personal universe, and therefore in control of what happens in it. I did have an idea, however dim, of a Greater Power, or Force for good being out there somewhere, and looking for me, but it wasn't quite part of my life's journey.'

At this time, she was keenly aware that the children needed a father in their lives, although she didn't hold out much hope of ever finding a supportive partner for herself. When she met her third husband, who was also looking for family life, she thought her troubles were over.

'I became pregnant almost straight away, and we planned to marry at some point. But he was involved in drug dealing, and was arrested and imprisoned for three and a half years. Sadly, we also lost the baby before full term. Those years went by in a whirlwind of prison visiting; we got married while he was in prison, and I felt completely consumed by the

> **" He was involved in drug dealing, and was arrested and imprisoned for three and a half years. Sadly, we also lost the baby before full term. "**

necessity of supporting my husband, and trying to preserve some kind of normal family life for the children. It was in endeavouring to maintain equilibrium for them that I found the strength to keep going. My idea of God playing any part in our lives was now alien to me; I felt it was up to me, and me alone.'

When finally the prison term was served, I assumed we would pick up the pieces and start again. What I hadn't reckoned on was the trauma and disorientation of returning to family life. Having spent so little time together, the marriage couldn't survive the pressures of that estrangement. With no spiritual bonds to hold to us together either, we parted after three more years.

> **" After each parting, I have felt enormous sadness and a sense of failure in not being able to hold things together. "**

'After each parting, I have felt enormous sadness and a sense of failure in not being able to hold things together. How naïve and even arrogant I was to suppose I could sort it all out without God. I decided to go back to work to support the children through school and university.'

It was while her son was at university that he became a Christian. Linda was amazed, confused and intrigued. During the holidays when he came home, Linda started to accompany him to church. He thought she might enjoy it, which she did, to her surprise.

'There was such an open-hearted welcome and acceptance, that I continued to go for myself. There was a lot I had to be thankful for – my children married, and I now have three grandchildren – yet there was always something missing. Could there really be a connection between man and God, between God and me?

'I had to admit that my attitude to Christianity was changing, and although still unconvinced by the theology, I welcomed the support of the church family. I was encouraged to join something called Christianity Explored,* where we asked our questions informally while having something to eat, with our Bibles open and discovering who Jesus was.

'I enjoyed it intellectually, but it left me wondering what came next. I was in a bit of a vacuum, unable to commit, and beginning to feel hypocritical by still attending church. Then one Sunday morning, during a sermon entitled "Are you a Christian?", I realized I had run out of reasons to say no. So mentally kicking and screaming, I had to decide to take steps so I could say yes.

'I finally understood that I needed God's gift of forgiveness, and I admitted it. That was the huge shift for me – to really be open to God's love. There was nothing that I have done that could have deserved such a gift. Despite my church background as a child, I don't recall ever having had the concept of God's love being so great that He would take on human form, live a blameless life, be tortured, die on the cross, and then rise from the dead, all so that I could be right with God and at peace with Him. Amazing!'

> **" I finally understood that I needed God's gift of forgiveness."**

* Linda found the Christianity Explored group helpful when she had so many questions about God and faith. Maybe you would be interested in finding out more about a group in your area.

Visit: **www.christianityexplored.org**
or any of the contact addresses at the end of this book.

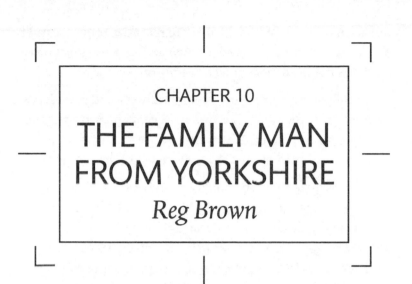

CHAPTER 10
THE FAMILY MAN FROM YORKSHIRE
Reg Brown

Brass bands and rugby league are a couple of the things that might come to mind when you think of Yorkshire. The largest county in England is full of abbeys, dales and moors, former coalfields, and has a long coastline. From Pomfret Cakes in Pontefract (for the uninitiated, these are liquorice sweets) to the rhubarb from the sheds near Wakefield, to wonderful cakes and pastries served with Yorkshire Tea at 'Betty's' in Harrogate, food features strongly throughout the region. Bradford's kormas, curries and poppadoms now vie with fish and chip shops to top the list of Yorkshire's most famous food. And I haven't even mentioned the delights of roast beef and Yorkshire pudding ... !

But a true Yorkshireman is the county's finest asset. 'True grit, 'allus calls a spade a spade', proud, hardworking, talented are some of the expressions which come to mind when describing 'tykes'. Famous men from the past include John Wycliffe, the first man to translate the Bible into English, William Wilberforce, the social reformer and politician who was instrumental in the abolition of the slave trade and, more recently, Arthur Scargill, the trade unionist and Freddie Trueman, the ferocious bowler who was the scourge of many a visiting cricket team.

Another type of 'tyke' who is less well known and yet deserves admiration is the quiet, hardworking gentleman of principle who people respect greatly, whilst not receiving great public acclaim or celebrity status. Mr Brown fell into this category.

When Reginald Brown took his first breath of Yorkshire air in Morley maternity hospital on 31 May 1923, he could, talent permitting, and if and when that tiny body matured, also be allowed to play county cricket for Yorkshire. (This rule has now been relaxed.) However, this was not to be, as Reginald's talents lay in other directions, and politically there were going to be dark days ahead. 'War clouds' were looming ominously.

> **" When the devastating news came that the country was at war, every family was affected. "**

He attended Churwell school until he was 14. Joinery was his favourite subject, but his first job was as an errand boy at Stone Bros., one of many bespoke tailors in Leeds. When the devastating news came that the country was at war, every family was affected. Lives were turned upside down by shortages of basic necessities, separation from loved ones, and tragedy. Hardship, sadness and fear were commonplace. It has been left to the newsreels, amateur photographers, journalists, historians and filmmakers to portray what it was really like to be a country at war. But nothing can compare with the actual eyewitness accounts of those terrible days. Young men such as Reginald went to serve their king and country, not knowing if they would ever return.

Reginald was called up to the navy in March 1942. He travelled at first to Ipswich to train at Shotley on board *HMS Ganges*, which was a land training boat. One of the more curious rules was that sailors had to climb up the ship's mast to the flagpole before being allowed to go on leave. Determination and the thought of home no doubt helped many a man scale those dizzy heights.

Before long, Reginald received the news that he was being sent to Gibraltar. This was where the British fleet had been given the task of stopping the Germans and Italians getting through the Strait of Gibraltar, which connects the Atlantic to the Mediterranean Sea. Until the advent and perfection of radar, this was a problem for the Allies. Spain, being a neutral country, continued to send its fishing vessels into the waters there at night. The British fleet had to plot every ship and make sure no spy boats slipped through.

VE Day came at last, giving rise to partying all over the country. Reg remembers that there was only one pub in Morley that had not run out of beer. He married the love of his life the day after, on 9 May.

There had been four Brown brothers, but only Reginald survived into old age. Albert died of pneumonia, aged 32 years. Sydney was killed during a Lancaster bomber raid over Germany. He was only 23 years old. Roy was in the RAF after the war, but was killed in a car crash aged 24 while coming home on leave.

Reg had a family, three girls and a boy.

'Dad was a very practical man and a great father. He could turn his hand to anything. As well as making toys, including a doll's house, he also made clothes,' remembers Jacqui, one of his daughters.

There was always plenty of time to play with his children. Reg would take them out at weekends even though he worked long hours, first at a leather works in Churwell for 27 years, then at Wm. Smith Ltd., dyers in Morley for 12 years. Even then he managed to squeeze into his busy life hobbies and interests such as gardening, DIY, crosswords, jigsaws and reading. He also kept a daily log of England's erratic weather, and read books about the subject in general. He was a 'gadget man' even when he was in his eighties. His grandson, Simon, often referred to him as 'My high-tech granddad'.

> **" War had made an immense impact on their lives, whether or not they had been on the frontline. "**

A great deal of men of his generation kept their thoughts about religion to themselves, and for a variety of reasons. War had made an immense impact on their lives, whether or not they had been on the frontline. Maybe they had questions that lay hidden, unuttered both to God and people. Or perhaps deep down there was a quiet belief that was not outwardly expressed. One thing was sure: In Reg's life, his family was extremely important to him.

Jacqui shared part of this private side of his life at Reg's funeral in 2010. 'My dad passed away on 8 March, aged 86. He and I were always close. He took good care of me as a child, and again in later life when my husband died very young leaving me with a young child to raise alone. I became a Christian aged 13. Dad was always impressed by my Christian friends, even though he himself did not attend church. When I had to spend a year in Germany as part of my degree course at university, Dad asked if I would be able to find a group of Christians like the ones he had met because then he would know that I would be safe and happy. He wouldn't have to worry about me. It was after my husband died suddenly of cancer that both my parents started to come to church with me. This was because again they were both impressed by the love and support which my son and I received from our "Christian family".

'Dad was a very private and quiet man who did not speak openly about such private matters as faith and belief in God. However, at the end of one Sunday morning service, after taking communion, Dad asked me to explain what had been said from the pulpit "that only those who had received Jesus into their hearts as their own personal Saviour should take communion". Upon hearing what I had to say by way of explanation, Dad told me that he would no longer partake of communion. I was naturally upset as Dad was telling me in his own honest way that he wasn't a Christian. However, he still accompanied me to church.

'I can't remember now if months or a year or two passed when I was taken by surprise to see dad take part in communion. When I asked him about this, he was overcome with emotion and unable to speak about it. However, on the way home, he told me that he had been listening to the Sunday morning religious programme on BBC Radio 2. There had been an interview with a politician, John Major, who had said during the course of the conversation that you shouldn't wait until you felt you understood everything to put your trust in God. This was clearly what Dad needed to hear, and something changed in Dad.

'Dad had always believed in God. He saw something very different in my life and the lives of my Christian friends. Perhaps he felt he couldn't be like them or me. Clearly, God spoke to him that day and enabled him to come very simply to God in his own way, just as he was.'

There is an old hymn that was very popular in post World War Two years, which resonated with many at that time; putting into words many private feelings that people had, but did not know how to express to God. It has helped folk such as Reg come to faith in Christ, trusting in Him alone for forgiveness and new life even in latter years:

Just as I am without one plea
But that Thy blood was shed for me,
And that Thou bidst me come to Thee,
O Lamb of God, I come, I come.

Just as I am, and waiting not
To rid my soul of one dark blot,
To Thee whose blood can cleanse each spot,
O Lamb of God, I come, I come.

Just as I am, though tossed about
With many a conflict, many a doubt,
Fightings and fears within, without,
O Lamb of God, I come, I come.

Just as I am, Thou wilt receive,
Wilt welcome, pardon, cleanse, relieve;
Because Thy promise I believe,
O Lamb of God, I come, I come.

Just as I am, Thy love unknown
Has broken every barrier down;
Now to be Thine, yea, Thine alone,
O Lamb of God, I come, I come.*

* 'Just as I Am, Without One Plea', Charlotte Elliott, 1789–1871.

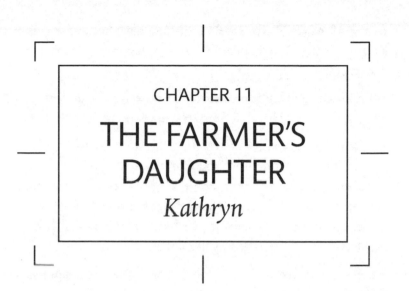

CHAPTER 11

THE FARMER'S DAUGHTER

Kathryn

Hill farming is not for the faint-hearted. Hill farmers are a special breed. They have to be. The climate forces them to have tough skin, stamina and real determination to eke out a living in the remote terrain. When Kathryn was born in the early 1900s, she entered a difficult and harsh environment and a troubled world, plus a country that would soon be at war yet again.

Farm life was typical of those days, with hard work inside and out, and the Bible very much in evidence in the home. Although Kathryn's parents had probably come under the influence of the 1904 Welsh revival, she admits that she cannot claim with any certainty that they were true Christians, even though they were 'chapel' people. Her memories are not predominately happy, but rather of austerity and fear.

She recalls: 'I had been introduced to, and grown up with, a vindictive God – someone "out there" who was constantly watching and waiting, ready to pounce if ever I put a foot wrong. However, some good seed must have been sown, as I clung on to this God that I didn't know, often crying out to Him in desperation to help me.'

But it was to be a long time before she came to really understand who God is, what He is like, and to know Him personally.

When a girl left school back then she was expected to take up her duties at home until she married. Kathryn had had no grand ideas of a career. Her mother was not strong so she had to become, in effect, her father's housekeeper. The family expected it. The community expected it. Her brother, meanwhile, had to be educated and supported by her father.

Kathryn married at an early age. Unfortunately any happiness from the marriage was short-lived. Within a few years, her husband had left her with two very young children to support.

'Without job or income I had no option but to return to my parents. Life became very difficult. I was desperate for a home of my own. Months rolled into years and still there was no prospect of living an independent life.'

Kathryn had no access to the benefit system such as we know it today. Single parent families had no rights, despite their responsibilities and regardless of their circumstances.

Innocent parties were perceived as guilty with little mercy shown. Women such as Kathryn had no means of support, limited education, and no training.

'But God was not about to give up on me. He was going to answer my cries for help. It had to be God, because in the natural world the odds were so heavily stacked against me,' she says. 'I had heard that a local council house had become available, so along with twenty-five others, I applied for it. I also asked God for it. Miraculously, and out of the blue, it was mine, and it is mine to this day.'

The years went by. Her two boys became young men who married and had their own families. One left Wales to settle in the USA.

Kathryn was on her own again. Life's trials had left her with little spiritual appetite. She would perhaps attend the requisite Easter and Christmas chapel services and maybe drift in to church at other times of the year, but there was nothing to hold her.

'The religion I grew up with, and sporadically continued in, was cold and unloving. The pain resulting from my husband's desertion went very deep. I felt alone in the world, especially when my parents died and my focus was on providing a home for my two boys. But once they had left the nest, the feeling of loneliness bit even deeper. Yes, I met people at work, but they always stayed on the periphery of my life. Me against the world; that's how I felt. Alone and unloved, I withdrew inwardly.'

When the opportunity arose, Kathryn bought her house from the local authority. This step brought a purpose to her life. Progressively, she made improvements, both inside and out, as money allowed. And as Kathryn explains, 'It was to be God's pathway for bringing me to Him.'

One of her projects was to build a wall at the front of the property, with steps up from the road. Kathryn enlisted the help of a local tradesman, but he was too busy to be able to create a pathway and additional steps higher up the garden. Impatient to get the work completed as soon as possible, Kathryn tried everywhere to find a workman, to no avail.

'I cried out to God to help me; to provide me with someone to complete the job.'

One day, she noticed a small advert in the village shop advertising the services of a gardener/handyman. 'This has to be worth a try,' she thought, so she made contact and arranged a meeting. Two months later, Tony started the work. With the work finished, and chatting over a cup of tea in the kitchen, Kathryn began confiding in Tony about her son in America who had become a constant worry. He had marriage problems and had been drinking heavily for some considerable time.

'I made the comment that I thought my son needed to get in touch with a good counsellor in order to sort himself out. The reply I was given was not one I expected.

"Your son doesn't need a counsellor, he needs Jesus!" Upon which he proceeded to share with me how he himself had found a new life in Jesus Christ. We then began to talk about spiritual things.' It was the start of a conversation that was unique for her. 'Tony told me how he now had a relationship with God, who he had never known before, despite having been brought up in the church. I told him that for many years I had been crying to God, and that I wanted to know Him. I knew He was out there somewhere, but where? How could I find Him? He was so distant.

'Tony told me that my problem was the problem common to everybody – that our sin was a barrier to finding and knowing God. I was assured that He was very near, so near that all I had to do was to take a simple step of faith. I needed to repent of my sin and life of rebellion towards God, ask for His forgiveness, and trust in the finished work of Christ – His death and resurrection, completely surrendering my life to Him.' She was understanding that Jesus had taken the punishment for all our wrong so that we can be made right with God.

Continuing, she says, 'When, some days later I next saw Tony, I told him that I had taken this step. That was back in the summer of 2003. From that day, my life changed. I was never one for reading, but immediately I had this tremendous appetite for the Bible and books about Jesus. I am now in a living, loving relationship with God and am learning to trust Him with my life. I have a constant Friend in Jesus who never leaves me. Inwardly I used to be in turmoil and often rage at situations. Now I have found peace, patience and eternal life in Jesus.'

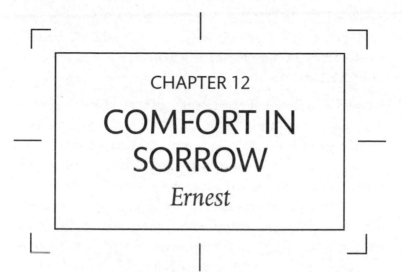

CHAPTER 12

COMFORT IN SORROW

Ernest

In life we shall encounter an unwelcome visitor to our home. This intruder is expected, but with no exact time of arrival. This enemy also brings sorrow and pain with it. Uninvited and unwanted, death is that visitor.

Ernest was very bitter and angry, something he readily admitted. Standing at the graveside of his beloved Bobbie at Fulwood, Sheffield, he felt totally shattered and full of grief. The loss of his wife, who had been snatched from him unexpectedly at the age of 70, was a cruel blow and left a big hole in his life. Only three weeks later, his dear mother passed away also. 'This was too much! I soon became a very unsociable grouch.'

> **" Standing at the graveside of his beloved Bobbie at Fulwood, Sheffield, he felt totally shattered and full of grief. "**

But Ernest had to somehow carry on. The everyday things still had to be attended to, and meals prepared. Saturday was fish and chip day. On his way to the local chip shop, Ernest would talk regularly to a lady, who in conversation would often mention the Christ Church Friday Club.

Ernest's background was not one of a regular churchgoing kind, although his mother had been brought up in a church orphanage. Probably because of this, she decided that her son would be confirmed. Ernest took confirmation classes in 1936 partly at Ranmoor Church and partly at Christ Church vicarages. Following his confirmation, he did not attend church. In fact he does not recollect his parents going either, except for weddings and funerals. Along came the war years, during which he served in the RAF at home and abroad. After being demobbed in 1947, a young lady, the daughter of family friends, caught Ernest's eye. Barbara, or Bobbie, as he affectionately called her, had been working in the Land Army and lived only a few doors away. Bobbie and Ernest married at Ranmoor in 1949.

> **" At the Friday Club they didn't know what to do with the unsociable man who didn't play board games, cards, snooker or bowls. Hence I was sent off to read the papers! "**

Now, after all those years and grieving the loss of his wife, a very insistent lady was inviting him to some church club. Although not very interested or enthusiastic, Ernest was eventually 'bullied' into going.

'At the Friday Club they didn't know what to do with the unsociable man who didn't play board games, cards, snooker or bowls. Hence I was sent off to read the papers!'

One Friday, someone found Ernest in tears. 'Without more ado she led me by the hand into the church, prayed out loud and just sat quietly. I had a great feeling of peace and tranquillity. It was a strange emotion for me.

'Anyway, I continued attending the Friday Club and was still an unsociable old grouch. One of the young helpers – only a teenager – used to come over and talk to me. Bit of a nuisance at the time, until one week she said to me, "You know your Bobbie is in the graveyard … will you take me to see her?" Not to see her *grave*, which other people had said. This missing word made it seem different and special, and afterwards I was really looking forward to our Friday chats.' The helper was a young trainee with the church. She and Ernest and became good friends, but he still did not go to church.

Inevitably his new friends, or 'minders' as he referred to them, posed the question, 'Have you thought of going to a Sunday service?' 'Needless to say, my two minders had their way, and I was collected and taken to the Sunday service by the trainee who sat the old man with her young friends, in the balcony next to the organ.'

Ernest continued to attend regularly, sitting as always in the same seat. But every time it came to the Communion Service he was concerned and embarrassed, for even though he had been confirmed all those years ago, he did not feel totally committed. Among the many meetings planned for all ages and levels of interest, this church organized an 'Open to Questions and Open to Answers' course. Ernest talked endlessly to everyone there, including the minister, Reverend Hugh Palmer. 'He convinced me to stop worrying, as he knew I was giving a lot of thought and consideration to the problem, and it would, in time, be resolved.

> **" I just felt it was time, for I recognized that I believed the truths mentioned in the words of consecration. "**

'This did eventually happen at the beginning of a Communion Service. After the Creed and the minister's introduction I just felt it was time, for I recognized that I believed the truths mentioned in the words of consecration. But being the world's best at procrastination, I thought I would leave it until next time. However, it was mentioned that I was a little apprehensive and somewhat embarrassed, so come the next Communion Service the trainee took my hand and led me down from the balcony to take communion.

'An old man, hand in hand with a young female – but that hand held so tightly gave me such great confidence. As we approached the rail at the front of the church, the minister was standing there with a faint smile on his face, and just as we passed he gave us a wink ... yes, a wink! And with that, all my apprehensions vanished, and I took my first communion. Afterwards I looked at what was a blur of faces in the congregation. A blur because I had a tear or two in my eyes; not tears of anger, pain or sorrow now, but tears of joy because I felt I was really a member of *this* church family. It was only a little later that I thought, "No, not *this* church family, but also the *wider* family of God."

'Through my faith, I hope I am a different person to that bitter old grouch I had become before the episode in that chip shop. I now enjoy the company of others, and always feel that if I do have a problem, there is always someone I can talk to and pray with.' Ernest had trusted Jesus as his Lord and Saviour. He found the truth of the words from the Bible, 'if you confess with your mouth, "Jesus is Lord," and believe in your heart that God raised him from the dead, you will be saved' (Rom. 10:9).

Ernest died and went to be with His Lord in 2010.*

* If you would like a free copy of the booklet, *Comfort in Times of Sorrow*, please get in touch via the contact address at the back of this book.

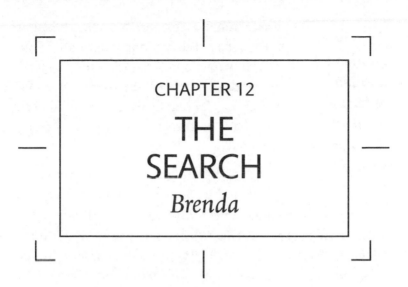

CHAPTER 12

THE SEARCH
Brenda

Have you ever built your family tree? Research can be time consuming, expensive and sometimes frustrating, but is carried out with the anticipation of discovering someone in your family with an intriguing story.

Brenda is a searcher. She loves to find out about all sorts of things. When she embarked on tracing the generations of her family she never dreamed just how far she would go back. Now in her seventies, Brenda's search through records has taken her to the staggering early date of AD 870.

The fact that she can go so far back probably means that her ancestors were landed gentry. There are also descendants recorded in the Doomsday Book. Relatives had owned most of East Anglia as well as property in Norwich, and included three mayors. A connection with royalty was discovered when, in later years, a woman called Sophia, who originally came from Suffolk, ended up in London. Desperately looking for work, she was granted a position as kitchen maid at Buckingham Palace. Sophia not only found herself a new and interesting life but also, alongside hard work, discovered love and romance. Thomas Brown, one of Queen Victoria's coachmen, caught her eye and captured her heart.

Brenda was delighted to read of her great-grandmother, Sophia. Living in the days of the Empire, the young couple must have had great hopes and much excitement as they married and set up home at 37 North Street in Marylebone, London. Three children arrived in due time bringing further happiness. Life expectancy was shorter than today, but nevertheless it was with great sorrow and dismay that Thomas died when Sophia was only 40. She took her children first to Lowestoft, where relatives were fishing folk involved in the herring trade. From there she went by boat up to South Shields where her brother lived.

Brenda's search for information entered a new phase, with her own memories filling in gaps on the family tree. She remembers quite clearly living partly in Yorkshire and then later in Northumberland in a little two-bedroom stone cottage. Her grandmother lived with the family; she was a staunch Methodist lady.

'There was a large kitchen-cum-living room, but no scullery or washing facilities – only a pantry. The lavatory was open and outside. Men would call at 12 o' clock to empty the "midden". Everything was so muddy. The young and old women together would hang out their washing on lines across the street. In those days, all the groceries were delivered by horse and cart, so the women had to dash out and hoist up the numerous washing lines with wooden props so that the delivery man could get through. Times were hard in the mining village.

'My dad died when I was only 11. He contracted silicosis, the miner's disease affecting the lungs, through working at the stone colliery. He developed cancer, taking a year to die. Tragically, back then, all that could be done for the men was to

> **" My dad died when I was only 11. He contracted silicosis, the miner's disease affecting the lungs."**

take them home, where they stayed until they passed away. I remember my grandmother speaking to my atheist dad as he lay dying, urging him to put his trust in God. I constantly worried about my mother who was never well and lost her faith due to watching her husband die a long, painful death. But I prayed every night with my grandma before going to sleep. I even became a Sunday school teacher.'

Eventually the pit was closed, followed by the demolition of the stone houses. Families were rehoused, and Brenda found herself living at Newbiggin by the Sea. She met a man whom she married, and gave birth to three children. But things didn't turn out as she had expected. This man filled her life with abuse and fear for the next nineteen years until she ran away, searching for a better life for herself and the children. Brenda took up nursing and met her second husband, with whom she had a daughter. They lived in Derby, where they both had jobs in hospitals.

Although she was more settled she was still, in her heart, searching for something. She joined a local church but she found no fellowship there. When she tried to read the Bible she found it confusing and hard to understand. 'I was always searching. I

"I was even more lost." read the Qur'an. I also spent a day with nuns. I travelled up to the Holy Island of Lindisfarne, which I found very peaceful.' And yet, she was still searching. Back in Derby, Brenda had a friend who was a Jehovah's Witness. She invited her to go along to the Kingdom Hall. They too were of no help in her search. 'I studied with them for a year,' says Brenda, 'but I was even more lost.'

It was her daughter who was instrumental in leading Brenda to a place where her long search ended and, as well as finding answers to her questions, she made the biggest discovery of her life.

It was Christmas 2008 when Sharon invited Brenda along to a special candlelit carol service at Stenson Fields Christian Fellowship in Derby. Right from the start, she knew she had come 'home'. After the service, there was an invitation for people who wanted to know more about becoming a Christian or had any questions, to go along to a 'Just Looking' group once a week. Brenda joined with anticipation. Her search was nearly over.

"The puzzle was complete. What I discovered was so simple." 'There were all the answers that I had looked for. The puzzle was complete. What I discovered was so simple. Jesus wanted me to come to Him, confess my sins, and let Him into my life. Why did it take me so long?'

Religion had not been the answer, but rather a relationship found in Jesus Christ alone. He calls each of us to come to Him.

Brenda's husband had never read the Bible. She, on the other hand, was rapidly devouring it now that it made sense. They started going along to church together, and slowly things began to change in his heart and life too. They started to read the Bible together, finding out more about the God who loved them so much that He sent His Son to die in their place to pay the price for their sins.

> *" Another Christmas drew near with all the usual hectic preparations, presents and partying."*

Another Christmas drew near with all the usual hectic preparations, presents and partying. Brenda and her husband managed to find time to go along to church on Christmas Day, where he received the greatest gift of all. Many shed a tear as this father and husband trusted Jesus Christ as his Lord and Saviour at that service.

Faith is precious and personal, but what about when it is tested? Brenda had faced difficulties before, but now while in her late seventies she was about to hear devastating and heartbreaking news.

'In August 2010, my daughter, who was a head teacher, and her family went on holiday to an island in Scotland. The day before they were due to come home they were travelling along the A816 to Oban to a country park, when someone driving a Kia 4x4 vehicle hit them head-on at great speed on their side of the road. My daughter, her daughter, her boyfriend, my son-in-law and my great-granddaughter were airlifted by two helicopters to a hospital in Glasgow to the Intensive Care Unit. It was a broken family, literally. They all had suffered fractured bones but were alive. Three weeks later, having been on a ventilator, my daughter came home. After two days she felt very unwell and was in a lot of pain. I dialled 999. She died in the ambulance on her way to hospital.

'I could easily have blamed God and lost my faith, but God remains in my heart. He has given me the strength to go on and a loving church group who, like Him, have not left us alone or ignored us, but who have always been at our side to help, care and support us.'

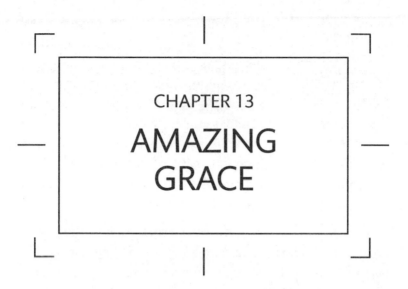

CHAPTER 13

AMAZING GRACE

I guess being lost is one of the most frightening experiences we might ever have to face. It could be anywhere and at any age. Being found, on the other hand, would be an exhilarating, overwhelming moment that would always be fixed in our memories.

Many years ago, a man called John Newton wrote some words about being 'lost' and then 'found' by God. We know the song as 'Amazing Grace'. Although his conversion was not in old age, his life is a graphic illustration of God's grace to humankind.

John's mother did the best she could for him. It was the early eighteenth century. Being a pious woman, she taught him to read the Scriptures, and memorize catechisms and hymns from an early age. But sadly she died when John was only seven. John's father was a sea captain who provided more distant care and was certainly less religious. He took the boy John, when only eleven, to sea. Over the next few years he was given a stern and

> "John did make his mark on the English parliament in Westminster, but not in the way his father probably envisaged."

thorough education in seamanship. No doubt his father had high ambitions for his boy, as good money could be earned criss-crossing the seas with cargoes of slaves. Maybe one day he would own a planter's estate, which in turn might even earn him a place in parliament as an MP. John did make his mark on the English parliament in Westminster, but not in the way his father probably envisaged.

John soon descended into the typical low life of a sailor of that period. But somewhere amid this harsh way of life he managed to fall in love with a girl called Mary who was the daughter of family friends. Unfortunately, a cruel press gang found him and carted him off to a man o' war of the Royal Navy. There followed the terrible process common to that time period whereby many young men were subjected to severe discipline, floggings and near starvation until they were 'broken'. All this was to enable them to serve and survive in the Royal Navy when at war and dealing with the elements.

Eventually John escaped, but only to end up fully involved with the cruel slave trade. Slaves would be loaded and packed, chained side-by-side, row after row, often up to six hundred souls. If they survived the journey they would be traded for sugar and molasses to manufacture rum.

On one memorable voyage aboard *The Greyhound* journeying from Brazil to Newfoundland something happened which was to change his whole life, and as a consequence was to affect thousands of other lives. A dreadful storm blew up. The ship began taking in water. Now there was real danger for him as he could easily be washed overboard, or the boat might even disintegrate. Into his head came all the remarkable deliverances he had had in the past, the extraordinary twists and turns; also his wayward lifestyle and how he had turned his back on God even to the extent of mockery. At first John thought that he had sinned too much to have any hope that God would forgive him. The storm did not abate. John really did think then that he was about to die. At that point he remembered that the Scriptures taught about grace; God's great love toward sinners. John cried out to God for help and mercy.

John did not die. He thought all was lost physically but was saved; and he thought all that had been spiritually lost but had been found by the Saviour who loved him and gave Himself for him. John Newton eventually turned away from the cruel slave trade, later to become a much-loved vicar. Along with his poet friend William Cowper, he enjoyed writing, especially hymns. A significant pamphlet was published by Newton entitled *Thoughts Upon the African Slave Trade*. He began with an apology and then described what he had seen in his time as a slave trader. A copy was sent to every MP. Newton was called to testify before parliamentary hearings about slavery. William Wilberforce, arguably the greatest social reformer Britain has seen, was greatly affected by the whole horrible traffic of people, resulting in him pressing for the abolition of the slave trade.

John Newton died in 1807, which was just nine months after parliament voted to abolish the slave trade in the British Empire. One of his most famous hymns 'Amazing Grace' is his own story, and has also become a legacy for succeeding generations, pointing people to the One who forgives and changes lives.

Amazing grace! How sweet the sound,
That saved a wretch like me!
I once was lost, but now am found;
*Was blind, but now I see.**

Translated into numerous languages, performed by brass bands, orchestras, organs and bagpipes, sung in cathedrals, prisons and by royalty, this song is a testimony to how John Newton found faith through grace – God's free, unearned favour.

At the age of 82 he wrote the following words that in years to come were picked up and uttered in the film *Amazing Grace* starring Ioan Gruffudd:

'My memory is nearly gone, but I remember two things: that I am a great sinner, and that Christ is a great Saviour.'

Not all of us have led such wicked lives as John Newton, although the Bible tells us that we all have sinned, but his story gives us all hope. The Bible teaches that we are all lost from God. There will be no peace or security until we are found. So we need the grace that God offers us. How then can we be 'found'?

* '*Amazing Grace*', John Newton, 1725–1807.

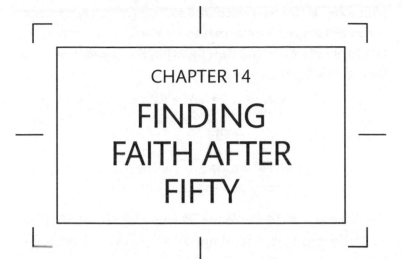

CHAPTER 14

FINDING FAITH AFTER FIFTY

Although we need to be 'found' it is equally important to be saved by the right person! We need to know that they can really get us to safety. It is so encouraging to know that God promises us that if we seek Him we will indeed find Him (see Jer. 29:13,14). On Christmas posters outside churches sometimes we read the slogan 'Wise men still seek Jesus'. To understand how we can find faith and have a personal relationship with God, we first have to consider Jesus Christ. In the Gospels, the first four books in the New Testament, we can read for ourselves about His birth, life, death and resurrection – we discover that He truly is the Son of God, the Messiah, and the Saviour of the world.

Jesus, who once was laid in a crib, was destined to die on a cruel cross. Hanging in humiliation and shame as He was crucified,

> **" Jesus, who once was laid in a crib, was destined to die on a cruel cross."**

Jesus took on Himself the sin of which we are guilty. He died as our substitute. As Saviour, He carried all our in on Himself. He died in our place so that we could be forgiven and reconciled to God. The Bible says:

> We all, like sheep, have gone astray, each of us has turned to his own way; and the LORD has laid on him the iniquity of us all. (Isa. 53:6)

> For Christ died for sins once for all, the righteous for the unrighteous, to bring you to God. (1 Pet. 3:18)

> He [Jesus] himself bore our sins in his body on the tree ... (1 Pet. 2:24)

But just as for a drowning person it is not enough simply to look at a lifebelt and believe it will save them, we actually have to commit ourselves to Jesus and 'grasp' Him, the means of being saved. As individuals we need to ask Jesus to forgive us. Because Christ not only died, but rose again from the dead, He is willing to become our Lord, Saviour and Friend. He sends His Holy Spirit to live within us, to keep us close to Him, and one day will take us home to be with Him for ever.

Heaven is not a reward, but a gift given to all who will simply receive Jesus by faith. This is God's grace to you and me. Whatever our past, and however we have previously thought about God, it is crucial to trust Jesus who invites us to Himself.

> Jesus said, 'Come to me, all you who are weary and burdened, and I will give you rest.' (Matt. 11:28)

> For the grace of God that brings salvation has appeared to all men. (Titus 2:11)

> For it is by grace you have been saved, through faith –

and this not from yourselves, it is the gift of God – not by works, so that no one can boast. (Eph. 2:8,9)

[Jesus Christ] came to seek and to save that which was lost. (Luke 19:10)

As you have read the stories of real people from differing backgrounds in different circumstances, you will have gathered that they have each found faith through Jesus Christ. He is the way, the truth and the life (see John 14:6).

Through Jesus we will find answers to our questions, comfort for our sorrows and fears, plus certain hope for the future. May I earnestly encourage you right now to pray to God for His mercy and grace; to pardon you for all your sin; and then thank Him and ask the risen, living Lord Jesus to come to live within your life. Ask Him to become your Lord, Saviour and Friend. Ask Him for His help to follow Him all your days.

He will hear and answer your prayer.

CONTACTS

If you would like to know more about the Christian faith, the Bible, or find a church, please contact:

Web: **www.10ofthose.com** or **www.tell-me-more.org**

Email: **roger@rogercarswell.com**

Or: **SAGAS, c/o Spring Cottage, Spring Road, Leeds LS6 1AD**

FURTHER READING

Comfort in Times of Sorrow, Roger Carswell
(10Publishing, Chorley, Lancs, 2012)

Grill a Christian, Roger Carswell
(10Publishing, Chorley, Lancs, 2011)

Live Wires, D.J. Carswell
(10Publishing, Chorley, Lancs, 2010)

Making the Most of the Rest of Your Life, John Chapman
(Matthias Media, Kingsford, NSW, 2007)

On My Way to Heaven, Mark Ashton
(10Publishing, Chorley, Lancs, 2010)

Real Lives, D.J. Carswell
(10Publishing, Chorley, Lancs, 2010)

Where is God in a Messed-up World?, Roger Carswell
(IVP, Nottingham, 2009)

MORE IN THIS SERIES

Real Lives *D.J. Carswell*
ISBN: 978-1-906173-32-6

Live Wires *D.J. Carswell*
ISBN: 978-1-906173-13-5

To place an order call: **0844 879 3243**
email: **sales@10ofthose.com**
or order online: **www.10ofthose.com**

a division of 10 of those.com

10Publishing is the publishing house of 10ofThose.
It is committed to producing quality Christian
resources that are biblical and accessible.

www.10ofthose.com is our online retail arm selling
thousands of quality books at discounted prices.
We also service many church bookstalls
and can help your church to set up a bookstall.
Single and bulk purchases welcome.

For information contact: sales@10ofthose.com
or check out our website: www.10ofthose.com